CABINET GOVERNMENT IN INDIA

CABINET GOVERNMENT IN INDIA

BY

R. J. VENKATESWARAN

LONDON
GEORGE ALLEN & UNWIN LTD
RUSKIN HOUSE MUSEUM STREET

C

242965

Politics.

PRINTED IN GREAT BRITAIN
in 11 point Juliana type
BY THE BLACKFRIARS PRESS LTD
LEICESTER

To My Mother

PREFACE

Since the Indian Constitution came into operation about sixteen years ago, many scholarly studies have appeared on various aspects of its working. But, so far as I am aware, no attempt has been made till now to analyse in detail the actual working of the Central Cabinet.

Michael Brecher, in his brilliant biography of Jawaharlal Nehru, has described the role of the Cabinet in Indian democracy but his treatment of this subject is brief. Moreover, his book was published about six years ago.

The book, *Leadership and Political Institutions in India*, edited by Richard L. Park and Irene Tinker, contains an interesting chapter on the Indian Cabinet of 1956. But it deals more with the human aspects of ministers than with their constitutional position. We are told, for instance, that nineteen ministers had a total of seventy-seven children of whom thirty-seven were sons and forty daughters.

The proper working of the Cabinet is of the greatest importance because on it depends largely the efficiency of administration and the progress of the country. There is at present a keen anxiety, on the part of the people in India and abroad, to know how the Indian Cabinet has been carrying on the affairs of the world's largest democracy. It will, therefore, be worthwhile to study to what extent the cabinet system, largely modelled on that of Britain, has taken root in India and how far we have been able to follow British precedents and conventions.

Although this book deals mainly with the working of the Indian Cabinet since the attainment of independence, I have given at the outset a chapter, explaining how the Central Government was carried on from the days of the Mauryan emperors to the time of Lord Mountbatten. The Mauryas, the Guptas, the Moguls and the British rulers did not have any cabinet system of government but the way they chose their ministers, allocated work, took decisions and conducted the administration, is of considerable historical interest.

My original intention was to write a book on the working of the Cabinet under Nehru. But by the time I completed the manuscript, Nehru died. I, therefore, decided to wait for some time until his successor had settled himself as the Prime Minister. Unfortunately, however, when the book was about to go to the press, came the sudden death of Lal Bahadur Shastri. The publication, therefore, was delayed a little but this has enabled me to include a chapter dealing with the election of Mrs Indira Gandhi. The book thus covers the working of the Cabinet under three Prime Ministers—Nehru, Shastri and Mrs Indira Gandhi.

I trust this book will help to focus attention on the strong and weak points of the Indian Cabinet and create a better understanding of the working of the most important organ of the Government of India.

My thanks are due to the staff of the National Library and the Library of the British Council, Calcutta, as well as to my friends who helped me in one way or the other in the preparation of this book.

I wish to add that the views expressed in this book are mine and do not necessarily represent the institutions with which I am connected.

R. J. VENKATESWARAN

Calcutta
October 15, 1966

CONTENTS

CHAPTER I

FROM MAURYAS TO MOUNTBATTEN

Chandragupta Maurya (322 B.C. - 298 B.C.) is generally regarded as the first historical emperor of India. His vast empire, with Pataliputra as the capital, covered the whole of North India and part of Afghanistan. He was a great warrior and vigorous ruler. We know a good deal of his administration from the writings of his adviser Kautilya who was a crafty statesman and shrewd observer.

The King was indeed all powerful. He was assisted by a council of ministers. In fact, from very ancient times, kings were always advised never to rule by themselves however strong and learned they might be. Authorities on Hindu law are unanimous in their emphasis on the need for ministers to guide, to warn and to encourage the kings.

Kautilya gives in his Arthasastra interesting details regarding the number of ministers a king should have, their qualifications, portfolios and the mode of consultation. 'All kinds of administrative measures', he says, 'are preceded by deliberation in a well-informed council.'

The important members of the council were the Prime Minister, the High Priest, the Treasurer-General and the Minister of War and Peace. The status of the Commander-in-Chief appears to have created a controversy which, according to Sir Percival Griffiths, 'strangely anticipated the dispute between Kitchener and Curzon more than two thousand years later'.[1] Some authorities consider the Commander-in-Chief as a minister. But others do not think so. Sir Percival says that Kautilya supports the latter view because he deals with the duties of the Commander-in-Chief along with those of the superintendents who were the official heads of the departments of the State and who

---

[1] *The British Impact on India* by Sir Percival Griffiths.

corresponded to the permanent under-secretaries in the British Civil Service.

There were other ministers in charge of various departments like agriculture, forests, commerce, customs, police, prisons and so on. There were also ministers without portfolios. The number of ministers varied from time to time.

The King might consult the ministers either individually or collectively. Kautilya suggests that the wise course would be to consult three or four ministers. 'Consultation with a single minister,' he says, 'may not lead to any definite conclusion in the case of complicated issues. A single minister proceeds wilfully and without restraint. In deliberating with two ministers, the king may be overpowered by their combined action or imperilled by their mutual dissension. But with three or four ministers, he will not come to any serious grief but will arrive at satisfactory results. With ministers more than four in number, he will have to come to a decision after a good deal of trouble. In accordance with the requirements of place, time and nature of the work in view, he may, as he deems it proper, deliberate with one or two ministers or by himself.'

What were the qualifications of ministers? Kautilya says that they should hail from noble families; they should be endowed with intelligence and imagination, eloquence and enthusiasm; they should be well trained in the arts and possess excellent character and free from such qualities as excite enmity. The loyalty of ministers was to be tested under religion, wealth, love and fear but 'never shall the king make himself or his queen an object of testing the character of his councillors'.

Great importance was attached to cabinet secrecy. The King was enjoined not to enter into deliberations in the cabinet meeting without taking effective precautions to ensure secrecy. The proceedings were to be so conducted that 'even birds cannot see them', for secrecy might be divulged by parrots, minas and other creatures.

As regards the relationship between the King and his Cabinet, opinion among scholars appears to be conflicting. Some hold the view that although the King might consult his ministers on important issues, he was free to accept or reject their advice. But there is a school of thought that suggests that cabinets took

14

decisions by majority vote and that the King had no alternative but to bow to them.

The Arthasastra says: 'When there is an extraordinary matter, the mantriparishad should be called and informed. In the meeting whatever the majority decide to be done, should be done by the King.' According to the Sukranitisara,

'without the *mantries* (Ministers), matters of State should never be considered by the king alone, he be an expert in all sciences and versed in policy. A wise king must always follow the opinion of the members of the council . . . He must never follow his own opinion. When the sovereign becomes independent of his council, he plans for his ruin. In fine, he loses the State and loses the subjects.'

The Brihaspatisutra says that kings were not free even to give gifts to the Brahmins without ministerial consent. There is also the interesting instance of King Rudradaman whose decision to repair the Sudarsana lake was opposed by his ministers. Consequently, the expenses had to be borne by the King himself from his privy purse.

While generally the kings in their own interest might have consulted their ministers on important matters, it seems difficult to agree with the view that the former had no freedom at all to act in their discretion. 'It is remarkable,' says K. P. Jayaswal, an eminent scholar, that 'the king is not given even the power of vetoing.' This conclusion appears rather far-fetched because, after all, the ministers were appointed by the king; they were responsible to him and to none else, and their office depended on his pleasure.

The Mauryan administration reached a high degree of efficiency during the time of Asoka (273 B.C. - 232 B.C.). He tried to establish a welfare State that sought to promote the happiness not only of the people but also of animals. His ministers were called Mahamatras and the Prime Minister was known as Agramatya.

Asoka introduced important changes in the administration. He set up a new department called the Ministry of Morals. Its duty was to work for the moral uplift of the people and to ensure that justice was administered properly. He made it compulsory for ministers to undertake frequent tours with a view to keeping personal contacts with the people. He paid special attention to improving the efficiency of the Public Works Department.

In Asoka's time, the people seemed to have understood the important distinction between obedience to the king and opposition to his ministers. This is clear from what the people of Taxila told Asoka's son who had been sent to that city on a mission of conciliation. 'We are not hostile to your Highness,' they said, 'or to King Asoka, but to the wicked ministers who insult us.'

Ministers continued to play an important part in the administration of the Gupta rulers (320 - 550 A.D.). Although the Guptas emphasised the divine character of kingship, they did not undermine the importance of ministers. In fact, the latter became more influential in this period and some of them made their office hereditary.

With the establishment of the Muslim rule in 1206 A.D. the authority of the kings increased enormously and that of the ministers declined. The kings behaved like despots, relying more on the strength of the military than on the popular will. Although occasionally a strong Prime Minister might assert himself, generally the kings had their own way. Even the Koranic law, which sometimes had a restraining influence on royal recklessness, was defied by powerful rulers like Allauddin. The people had no voice in the administration, the only remedies open to them being rebellion and assassination. All powers—executive, legislative and judicial—were concentrated in the king who was free to act as he liked.

Not all Muslim rulers, however, used their power arbitrarily. Akbar (1556 - 1605), the greatest of all of them, was an enlightened despot who strove hard to build up a united India. Although illiterate, he displayed administrative abilities of a high order.[1] His principal ministers were: the Vakil or Prime Minister, the Vizier or Finance Minister also called Dewan, the Chief Bakshi whose task included recruitment to the army and maintenance of

[1] Akbar's comment, quoted by V. A. Smith, on the competence of his ministers, is of considerable interest: 'It was the effect of the grace of God that I found no capable minister; otherwise people would have considered that my measures had been devised by him.'

certain registers, and the Sadr, the highest ecclesiastical officer. Apart from his regular ministers, Akbar consulted others like Abul Fazal who for many years acted as his most trusted adviser.

Aurangzeb (1658 - 1707), the last of the Great Moguls, was an able ruler but he was cruel and tactless and, by undoing the good work of Akbar, laid the foundation for the disintegration of the Mogul empire. The events that led to its break-up are not relevant to our study. What is important to note is that till the advent of British rule, the political situation in the country was confused and was not conducive to the growth of a sound administrative system.

ENTER BRITAIN

Conditions in India changed radically after the British had established themselves firmly. The maintenance of law and order, the spread of education, social reforms, and industrial expansion greatly facilitated the political unification of India. For the first time, this vast country came under a single administration which, by and large, was efficient and enlightened, and helped the evolution of the parliamentary system of government.

The important landmarks in the constitutional development of India may now be briefly summarized. In 1773 the British Parliament passed the Regulating Act. It made the Governor of Bengal the Governor-General of all British possessions in India. The Governor-General was to hold office for five years. He was to be assisted by a council of four members. He was also given the authority to control the administration of Bombay and Madras presidencies.

The Governor-General and his councillors were to decide all questions by a majority vote. The Governor-General was given a vote as well as a casting vote in case of a tie. But the Act did not work well because the councillors opposed Warren Hastings, the first Governor-General, on important matters. Deadlocks were frequent and good government became impossible. The Regulating Act was therefore amended in 1786. The Governor-General was given the power to override his council and function on his own responsibility in certain circumstances.

The Charter Act of 1833 raised the strength of the Executive

Council from three to four by the addition of a Law Member. But he could attend and vote only when legal questions came up for discussion. The Commander-in-Chief was made an extra-ordinary member of the Council and the Governor-General of Bengal was designated Governor-General of India.

The Charter Act of 1853 enhanced the powers of the Law Member who could now attend all meetings and vote on all questions.

The mutiny of 1857 brought about the end of the East India Company, and the administration of India was directly taken over by the British Government. A Secretary of State, assisted by a council, was appointed to look after the affairs of India. The Governor-General of India was also designated as Viceroy but he was to work under the direction of the Secretary of State for India. The Queen's proclamation of 1857, regarded for a long time as the Magna Carta of the people of India, helped to pacify and unify the country. It made the important announcement that public offices in India would be thrown open to all subjects without distinction of caste, colour and creed. Four years later was passed the Indian Councils Act. It raised the strength of the Viceroy's Executive Council from four to five with the addition of the Finance Minister. Another important change introduced by the Act was the adoption of the portfolio system. Prior to this, there was no proper division of work among the councillors. No member was given charge of any specific department. But under the portfolio system, as Dr A. B. Rudra observes, 'a member now ceased to be an adviser leisurely minuting in his own hand on papers referred to him and assumed the role of a responsible administrator of one of the great departments of the Government of India.' In 1874, a sixth member was added to the Council and he was given charge of the Public Works Department.

The Government of India Act of 1909, framed on the recom-mendations of Lord Morley, the Secretary of State of India, and Lord Minto, the Viceroy, was the next major landmark in the evolution of parliamentary democracy. The Act enlarged the membership and powers of the Imperial Legislative Council. Its members could now discuss the budget, move resolutions and ask questions and supplementary questions. But it was not permitted to discuss the affairs of the army and the Indian States. The legislative councils in the provinces were also widened and given more powers than before. For the first time an Indian member was appointed to the Viceroy's Executive Council and he was given the portfolio of Law.

The Act of 1909 did not however satisfy the political aspiration of the people of India though the moderate section of politicians welcomed the proposals. From the long-term point of view, the most serious feature of the Act was the introduction of separate electorates at the specific demand of certain leaders of the Muslim community. The argument of these leaders was that the Muslims constituted themselves into a separate community with a culture and a way of life different from those of the Hindus who were more numerous, more powerful and more prosperous than the other sections of the population. So unless the Muslims were given reserved seats and separate electorates, they could not be adequately and effectively represented in the legislatures. Their demand was readily conceded by the British Government.[1] The result was that communalism became an important factor in India's political life. The Muslim League came into existence in 1906 and, interestingly enough, the Hindu Mahasabha also was born in the same year. The Indian National Congress had been established in 1885 and its main objective in its earlier years was to achieve good administration and, in due course, self-government within the Commonwealth. From the very beginning, it had been a staunch champion of Indian unity but the introduction of separate electorates made the achievement of this goal difficult and ultimately led to the partition of India.

The Government of India Act of 1919 was in many respects a distinct improvement over the Act of 1909. Its main features were the following: The powers of the central and provincial Governments were clearly demarcated. The Central Government broadly confined itself to all-India affairs like defence, finance and communications. Subjects that were more or less of regional importance were given to provincial Governments. Bicameralism

[1] The Government of India, in recommending separate electorates, said in their communication to the Secretary of State for India in October 1908: 'The Indian Muhammadans are much more than a religious body. They form in fact an absolutely separate community, distinct by marriage, food and customs, and claiming in many cases to belong to a different race from the Hindus.'

was introduced into the central legislature. There were two houses—the Legislative Assembly and the Council of the State. The Assembly had a strength of 145 members of whom 105 were elected and forty nominated. The Council of State, mainly a revising body, consisted of sixty members—thirty-four elected and twenty-six nominated. The two chambers enjoyed co-equal powers in the matter of legislation. No major change was effected in the structure of the Viceroy's Executive Council. It continued to remain, as before, subordinate to the Secretary of State for India. But the fact that the Indian Legislative Assembly now consisted of a large number of elected and respected leaders from different parts of the country did have a beneficial effect on the central administration.

In the provincial sphere however the Act of 1919 made some far-reaching changes. It introduced what was known as dyarchy in the provinces. The provincial subjects were divided into two categories—reserved and transferred. The reserved category consisted of such vital subjects as finance, land revenue and law and order. These were in the hands of the British members of the Governor's Executive Council while the Indian members were given the charge of transferred subjects such as education, public health and agriculture. The provincial legislatures were further enlarged and the principle of direct election was introduced, the franchise being based mainly on property and residence in the constituency.

But the reforms of 1919 also failed to create any enthusiasm in the country. The substance of power was still in British hands. In fact, the authors of the reforms of 1919 themselves openly acknowledged their demerits when they remarked that 'hybrid executives, limited responsibility, assemblies partly elected and partly nominated, divisions of functions, reservations general or particular, are devices that can have no permanent abiding place.' Dyarchy in the provinces led to frequent deadlocks.[1] The

[1] 'What is the meaning of this system of dyarchy?' asked Colonel Yate in the House of Commons, and added, 'It is that in every province of India, however different the creeds and languages may be, you are to have two Executive Councils, one composed of British official members and the other of Indian unofficial members. These two Executive Councils are to be opposed to each other and to fight each other on questions affecting the Budget, the allotment of funds, and everything else.' Quoted by A. Appadorai in *Dyarchy In Practice*.

Indian ministers felt that they were unable to function effectively because the real power was not in their hands. It was only after the introduction of provincial autonomy under the Government of India Act of 1935 that the provincial governments came to have some substantial power. But this experiment did not last long because in 1939, on the outbreak of the second world war, the Congress ministries in the provinces resigned as a protest against India being dragged into the war without her consent. The Act had also envisaged the creation of a Federation at the Centre, consisting of the representatives of both British India and the Indian States. But this scheme did not materialize because of the opposition of certain influential Indian States. Moreover, the Act did not envisage the transfer of real power into Indian hands.

The detailed provisions of the Act of 1935 are not relevant to our study. What is important to note is that until August 15, 1947 the Executive Council of the Viceroy did not have the characteristics of a Cabinet. It was not responsible to the Indian legislature. Its members had no independence and could not take the initiative on important questions. Their loyalty was to the British Cabinet whose mandate it was bound to carry out implicitly. As Sir Henry Fowler, Secretary of State for India, explained,

'so long as any matter of administration or policy is undecided, every member of the Government of India is at liberty to express his opinion, but when a certain line of policy has been adopted under the direction of the (British) Cabinet, it is the clear duty of every member of the Government of India to consider not what that policy ought to be but how effect may best be given to the policy that has been decided upon, and if any member of that Government is unable to do this, there is only one alternative open to him and that is resignation.'

The Council also lacked homogeneity. Some of its members were officials, others were non-officials but without representative capacity. It was not surprising therefore that powerful Viceroys like Lord Wellesley, Lord Minto and Lord Hardinge practically ignored the Council. Indeed, Lord Ripon wrote to the

Secretary of State for India that the members of the Council were 'too amenable to the will of the Viceroy'. That was the true situation until India attained her freedom in August, 1947.

The Viceroy of India was not like the Governor-General of the Dominions. The Viceroy was endowed with vast and extraordinary powers. The Governor-General of the Dominions was a constitutional head like the British Monarch. But the Viceroy directly and actively participated in the Government of India. The Viceroy appointed councillors, distributed portfolios and he could override the decision of his council if necessary. He summoned, prorogued and dissolved the Central Legislature. He could extend its term beyond the prescribed period. He could prohibit the introduction in the legislature of any bill and also withhold his assent from any measure which, in his opinion, would be against British interests. If the legislature failed to pass a bill in the form recommended by him, he could enact it into law by virtue of his power of certification. Above all, he had the authority to issue ordinances without reference to the legislature.

In financial matters also the Viceroy had extensive powers. It was he who decided what items were to be classified as votable and non-votable. He could restore grants refused by the Assembly and authorise such expenditure as he thought necessary for the safety and tranquility of the British rule.

It must be emphasised however that even though the Viceroy's Executive Council never functioned as a Cabinet[1] and the Central Legislature enjoyed only limited powers, participation in these bodies gave Indians valuable experience that has stood them in good stead in free India. British rule in this country, despite its oppressive policies at times, was on the whole a liberal and progressive one. If today India, unlike many Asian nations, enjoys a stable democratic government, the credit must go largely to the British rulers who introduced their political institutions and conventions and built up an efficient administrative machinery.

Indians took to the parliamentary form of government with great gusto. The central legislature attracted some of the best brains of the country, and among its members there were many

[1] Lord Wavell tried in 1946 to convert the Executive Council into a Cabinet. But the attempt failed as we shall see in the next chapter.

leaders unrivalled for their deep learning and debating skill. In the early years of this century, for instance, the central legislature contained great statesmen like Gopal Krishna Gokhale, Surendranath Banerjee and V. S. Srinivasa Sastri. Under the Montford reforms, it included leaders of the eminence of Vithalbhai Patel, Motilal Nehru, Madan Mohan Malaviya, M. A. Jinnah and S. Srinivasa Iyengar. At a later stage, came veterans like Bhulabhai Desai and S. Satyamurthi. The last was one of the most brilliant parliamentarians of India, of whom Sir Percival Griffiths writes: 'Satyamurthi was perhaps the most practical and certainly the most industrious of all the Congress leaders in the Central Assembly. He read every white paper and blue book that appeared . . .'

The excellent training Indians received in parliamentary democracy helped to facilitate the transfer of power in 1947. By that time, British constitutional practices had taken root in India and when the time came to frame our Constitution, it was mainly to Britain that we looked for inspiration and guidance. Statesmen like B. R. Ambedkar, N. Gopalaswami Iyengar, Sardar Patel and K. M. Munshi, who dominated the Constituent Assembly, were admirers of the British Constitution and it was not surprising therefore that most provisions of the Government of India of 1935, framed by the British Parliament, were incorporated in the Indian Constitution.

So far as the Viceroy was concerned, it was only after the complete transfer of power in 1947 that he became the constitutional head of the Government of India. 'From today,' said Lord Mountbatten, in his historic broadcast to the nation on August 15th, 'I am your constitutional Governor-General and I would ask you to regard me as one of yourselves devoted wholly to the furtherance of India's interests.'

CHAPTER II

FIGHT FOR PORTFOLIOS

Before we proceed to study the working of the Cabinet in free India, it will be useful to analyse how the 'interim government', set up before the transfer of power, actually functioned. Although this Government lasted for hardly a year, the way in which it carried on the administration is of considerable political and constitutional interest. For the first time in the history of India, the representatives of the two most powerful political organisations accepted office at the centre and an attempt was made to convert the Executive Council into a real Cabinet. But the experiment failed because of the acute jealousies, suspicions and intrigues between the Congress and the Muslim League.

The interim government was formed on September 2, 1946. It was thought that a government consisting of popular representatives would be able to mobilize effectively the country's resources for tackling the great problems of post-war economic reconstruction. Lord Wavell, the Viceroy, referred to the formation of this Government as 'a very momentous step forward' on India's road to freedom. Although he did not agree to the demand of the Congress to keep his extraordinary powers in abeyance, he did assure them that the Government would be given the maximum freedom in the day-to-day administration.

The interim government at the beginning consisted of twelve ministers, namely: Jawaharlal Nehru, Vallabhai Patel, Rajendra Prasad, Sarat Chandra Bose, C. Rajagopalachari, Asaf Ali, John Mathai, Jagjivan Ram, Shafat Ahmed Khan, Baldev Singh, C. H. Bhabha and Ali Zaheer. The Congress took care to include the representatives of the Muslims, Christians and Parsees. But the Muslim League stood aloof for some weeks because it had not accepted the Cabinet Mission Plan for India's future constitutional set-up.

The members of the Government decided to work as a Cabinet with joint responsibility. They were called ministers and not members of the Executive Council as they had been designated before. It was believed that if they acted jointly, the Viceroy would find it difficult to interfere with their work. Interference with one would be tantamount to interference with all, and the entire Cabinet had decided to stand or fall together. Every evening the ministers used to meet informally under the leadership of Nehru to discuss important problems and arrive at tentative decisions. But when the League joined the Government on October 15, 1946, all hopes of converting the Executive Council into a Cabinet vanished.

The League sent five representatives to the Executive Council, namely Liaquat Ali Khan, Ghaznafar Ali Khan, Sardar Abdur Rab Nishtar, I. I. Chundrigar and Jogendra Nath Mondal, the last member representing the scheduled castes of East Bengal. Maulana Azad recalls in his autobiography how in selecting his nominees, Jinnah was careful to choose only those who would act as his yes-men. Thus Nazimuddin and Nawab Ismail Khan, who had been considered as certainties, were not included. Instead, Nishtar and Ghaznafar Ali Khan who, in the words of Maulana Azad, were 'dark horses about whom even members of the League had little information' were chosen. On the entry of the League, three representatives of the Congress, namely, Sarat Bose, Shafat Ahmed Khan and Ali Zaheer were dropped and the Council consisted of fourteen members.

Jinnah insisted that the most important portfolios should be equally distributed between the Congress and the Muslim League. Lord Wavell observed that in the existing conditions, all portfolios were of great importance and it was a matter of opinion which of them were the more important ones. Nevertheless, it is surprising to see how even experienced Congress leaders were outwitted by the League in the allocation of portfolios. The fight between the Congress and the League centred mainly around Finance and Home portfolios.

C. Rajagopalachari has interestingly described the situation thus: 'When the provisional Government was formed, we had a discussion among ourselves as to how the different ministries should be divided between the Muslim League and the Congress. Gandhiji was there. He did not know much about administration but he knew what was important. Jawaharlal was in a hurry to get things settled and he did not mind how. Liaquat Ali Khan wanted the Ministry of Finance and Vallabhai Patel wanted the Home Ministry. I was the only one with any real experience of administration. I said that the Ministry of Finance was not very important from a policy point of view because there were all sorts of necessary limitations on what could be done. But it had a lot of prestige attached to it and, therefore, it was good to make the concession to the Muslims. The Home Ministry also was not very important at that time because the real power was in the States. But I agreed that it was important from the point of view of prestige; and since Patel wanted it very badly, it was agreed by all of us that he should have it.'[1]

But subsequent events showed that the Congress, including Rajagopalachari, made a great mistake in agreeing to hand over Finance to the Muslim League. This gave opportunity to the League to interfere in every branch of the administration and obstruct the policies of the Congress. 'Whatever proposal was made by Sardar Patel,' writes Maulana Azad, 'was rejected or modified beyond recognition by Liaquat Ali Khan. His persistent interference made it difficult for any Congress member to function effectively.' Liaquat Ali Khan in his budget of February, 1946 imposed drastic and unprecedented measures of taxation with a view to crushing the power and influence of the Hindu capitalists, and the country took a long time to recover from the effect of these proposals.

The interim government never functioned satisfactorily. In fact, in the circumstances it was set up, it could hardly be expected to do so. 'The efficiency and prestige of the interim Government,' said Lord Wavell, 'will depend on ensuring that differences are resolved in advance of Cabinet meetings by friendly discussions. A coalition Government either works by a process of mutual adjustment or does not at all.' But from the very beginning Liaquat Ali Khan challenged Nehru's right to hold informal meetings and the League's representatives refused to attend them. Congress and League members met together only when the Viceroy called a meeting of the Cabinet. The League had already committed itself firmly to the demand for the division of India while the Congress was trying to avoid partition as far as practicable.

With such fundamental differences, it was not surprising that the interim government could not function as a cabinet. Liaquat Ali Khan frankly admitted that the government consisted of a Congress bloc and a Muslim bloc, each functioning under a separate leadership. Nehru said that the League had been attempting to establish itself as the king's party in the government; and Jinnah declared that the interim government was no more than the Viceroy's Executive Council under the Act of 1919, and that to call it a cabinet was a complete misconception. 'You cannot,' he said, 'turn a donkey into an elephant by calling it an elephant.' Indeed, the differences inside the Cabinet became so acute that the Congress members actually demanded the resignation of the League. But in the meantime, the British Government had announced their intention to divide and quit India by August 15, 1947. It was therefore decided to reallocate the portfolios in such a way that the Congress would be in charge of affairs relating to the Dominion of India and the League would take over the portfolios relating to Pakistan, while problems of common concern were to be dealt with jointly by both the wings under the chairmanship of the Governor-General.

CHAPTER III

QUINTESSENCE OF THE CONSTITUTION

Before we study the working of the Cabinet, it will be worth-while to analyse briefly the nature of the Indian Constitution and its main provisions. We have seen in the first chapter how parliamentary institutions came to be established in India after the advent of the British rule, and how Indian leaders enthusiastically adapted themselves to the new type of Government. It was therefore a relatively easy task for them to prepare a Constitution for their own country. The Constituent Assembly completed this task in about three years and the Constitution came into force on January 26, 1950.[1] Some idea of the enormous labour that went into its making will be clear from the fact that it consisted of 251 pages, 395 Articles, twenty-two Chapters and eight Schedules. It is a cosmopolitan Constitution in the sense that it incorporates certain aspects from the Constitutions of almost all the important countries of the world particularly from Britain, the USA, Eire and the Dominions. Above all, it has drawn heavily from the Government of India Act, 1935.

The Preamble to the Constitution proclaims India to be a Sovereign Democratic Republic. It makes it clear that the power of the Government is derived solely from the people of India and it promises to secure for them social, economic and political justice; liberty of thought, expression, belief, faith and worship; equality of status and of opportunity; and to promote fraternity, assuring the dignity of the individual and the unity of the nation.

The Constitution has enumerated in detail the Fundamental Rights of the citizens. These rights include equality before the law; prohibition of discrimination on grounds of religion, race,

[1] The Constituent Assembly held its inaugural session on December 7, 1946 and completed its task on November 26, 1949. But the Assembly continued to function as Parliament until the first general election was held in 1952.

caste, sex or place of birth; equality of opportunity in public employment; abolition of untouchability; protection of certain rights regarding freedom of speech as well as of life and personal liberty; prohibition of traffic in human beings, forced labour and employment of children in factories; right to freedom of religion; cultural and educational rights; right to property; and right to constitutional remedies. The Fundamental Rights have been included in the Constitution to protect the citizen against arbitrary action and discriminatory treatment by Government. The rights are enforceable in the courts; and the law-making authorities at the Centre and in the States are forbidden to enact measures in violation of these rights. But during times of national emergency, the rights may be suspended under the Constitution.

'Directive Principles of State Policy' are a unique feature of the Indian Constitution. These are not enforceable by any court. Nevertheless, they are, in the words of the Constitution, 'fundamental in the governance of the country and it shall be the duty of the State to apply these principles in making laws'.

The Directive Principles enjoin the State to promote the people's welfare by securing for them adequate means of livelihood, by equitable distribution of the ownership and control of the material resources, by preventing concentration of wealth and means of production to the common detriment, and by ensuring equal pay for equal work for women and men. Special care is to be taken to protect the interests of the weaker sections of the population particularly those of the Scheduled castes and Scheduled tribes. Further, the State shall endeavour to raise the level of nutrition and the standard of living of its people, and to bring about prohibition of the consumption, except for medicinal purposes, of intoxicating drinks and of drugs injurious to health. Finally, the State is called upon to promote international peace and security, maintain just and honourable relations between nations, foster respect for international law and treaty organisations, and encourage settlement of international disputes by arbitration. The incorporation of these Directive Principles has been criticized as being superfluous, ineffective and theoretical because nobody can compel the Government to observe them. Although this criticism may seem valid to some extent, it must be admitted that these principles do serve a useful purpose by setting forth laudable ideals to which no responsible Government can afford to remain indifferent.

The Government of India is a federation although this term is not used in the Constitution. The Constituent Assembly preferred the name 'the Indian Union' so as to emphasize the fundamental unity of the country. The powers have been distributed in such a way as to provide for a strong Centre. The subjects assigned to the Centre are indicated in the Union List consisting of seventy-seven items, the more important of them being defence, foreign affairs, currency and coinage, foreign trade, railways, posts and telegraphs, ports and airways, industries the control of which by the Union is declared by Parliament to be expedient in public interest, regulation of oil fields and mineral resources, organization of the Supreme Court and the High Courts and inter-State migration. The State List contains sixty-six items including public order, police, administration of justice, prisons, constitution and powers of municipal corporations, public health and sanitation, education, agriculture, land revenue, forests, fisheries and industries not controlled by the Centre. The concurrent list consists of forty-seven subjects including criminal law, preventive detention, marriage and divorce, civil procedure, economic and social planning, trade unions, social security, price control, factories, electricity, newspapers, books and printing presses. The Constitution also provides that, in the national interest, a subject in the State List can be transferred to the Union List for a period not exceeding one year provided the Rajya Sabha by a two-thirds majority approves of the proposal. A subject can also be shifted to the Concurrent List by a special procedure requiring the consent of legislatures of half the number of States. On subjects in the Concurrent List, both the Centre and States can legislate but the Central law can override that of the State in case of inconsistency. It will be thus seen that the Constitution has vested vast powers in the Centre, and the exigencies of planning in the last fifteen years have enormously strengthened it further.

The Indian Constitution is a flexible one. But being a written Constitution, it is not as flexible as that of Britain. Nor has it the rigidity of the American Constitution. The flexibility of the Indian Constitution is seen in the fact that till now it has been amended nearly twenty times.[1] The procedure for amendment is rather simple. An amendment can be initiated by introducing a bill for the purpose in either House of Parliament, and the amendment becomes law if passed in each House by a majority of the total membership of that House and by a majority of not less than two-thirds of that House present and voting; and it becomes valid after receiving the President's assent. But the amendment requires ratification by the legislatures of States in certain cases as, for instance, when changes are contemplated in the procedure for the election of the President or representation of States in Parliament. The Constitution is also flexible in another sense, namely, that in an emergency it can be converted almost into a unitary State with the President assuming extraordinary powers under Article 352.

THE UNION EXECUTIVE

The executive power of the Indian Union is vested in the President and is exercised by him through the Council of Ministers. The procedure for electing the President, his powers and functions and his relationship with the Council of Ministers are described in detail in chapter VII. Here it suffices to note that the Constitution provides for the parliamentary type of government chiefly on the model of Britain. The Council of Ministers consists of Ministers who are members of the Cabinet, Ministers of State who are not members of the Cabinet but hold Cabinet rank, and Deputy Ministers. The Council as such rarely meets. It is the Cabinet that meets frequently to decide policy matters.

The principal departments of the Government of India at present[2] are External Affairs, Home Affairs, Finance, Railways, Defence, Food and Agriculture, Steel and Mines, Education, Labour and Employment, Rehabilitation, Information and Broadcasting, Law, Petroleum and Chemicals, and Parliamentary Affairs and Communications. Each of these departments is under

[1] The *Statesman* of Calcutta, in an editorial in January 1965, observed: 'The Constitution has been amended on an average more than once a year; hardly an impressive record, especially when so many of the amendments have tended to deprive the ordinary citizen of existing rights and safeguards rather than, as in the American Constitution, to confer new rights.'

[2] This was the position under Shastri's premiership. For the distribution of portfolios under Mrs Gandhi see appendix.

a Cabinet Minister assisted, in some cases, by a Minister of State and a Deputy Minister. Some subjects like Commerce, Industry and Heavy Engineering, Health, and Irrigation and Power are in independent charge of Ministers of State. As regards Deputy Ministers, their main function is to assist the Ministers concerned both in Parliament and outside.[1] The Secretary is the administrative head of the Ministry. He is the chief adviser to the Minister. A Ministry has several divisions, branches and sections in charge of Deputy Secretaries, Under Secretaries and Section Officers respectively. To ensure the smooth functioning of the administration, the Constitution empowers the President, on the advice of the Prime Minister, to make rules and to allocate the subjects among ministers.

PARLIAMENT

The Indian Parliament is bicameral, consisting of the Lok Sabha or the Lower House, and the Rajya Sabha or the Upper House. The Lok Sabha represents the people and the Rajya Sabha the States. In ordinary law-making, the two Houses enjoy coequal power and in cases of disagreement between them, the President of the Republic is empowered to call a joint meeting. The question on which there is disagreement will be decided by a majority of members present and voting.

The Lok Sabha is more important, more powerful and more popular than the Rajya Sabha. The Lok Sabha consists of not more than 500 members elected directly by adult suffrage, all citizens of twenty-one years and above being entitled to vote, provided they are not otherwise disqualified. Provision is made for the reservation of seats for the Scheduled castes and Scheduled tribes and for the nomination of two representatives of the Anglo-Indian community. A member of the Lok Sabha must be an Indian citizen and not below twenty-five years of age. The duration of the Lok Sabha is five years. It has the right to elect

[1] A. K. Chanda writes in *Indian Administration*: 'Some Ministers make extensive use of Deputy Ministers, delegating most of the functions to them; others do not, allowing the Deputy Ministers merely to handle minor parliamentary work such as answering questions. Neither of these arrangements seems appropriate, and a *modus vivendi* has to be found, which will give the Deputy Ministers necessary experience without retarding government business or irritating the permanent officials.'

its chairman, called the Speaker, whose status and powers are more or less similar to those of the Speaker of the House of Commons.

The Lok Sabha is empowered to legislate on all subjects in the Union List as well as on those in the Concurrent List. It controls the executive by putting interpellations, by adjournment motions, by resolutions of no-confidence and, above all, by its power over the purse. All money bills originate only in the Lower House, a money bill being defined as one dealing with the imposition, abolition, remission, alteration or regulation of any tax; the regulation of the borrowing of money; the custody of the consolidated fund or the contingency fund and the appropriation of moneys out of such fund. And in case of a dispute as to whether a Bill is a Money Bill or not, the decision of the Speaker is final. After a money bill is passed by the Lok Sabha, it shall be transmitted to the Rajya Sabha. The latter shall return it with its recommendations within a fortnight, and the Lok Sabha may or may not accept them. The bill is then presented to the President for his assent.

The Lok Sabha has a number of committees to facilitate its work such as the Public Accounts Committee, Estimates Committee, Select Committees, Committee on Privileges, Rules Committee and Committee on Government Assurances. The Public Accounts Committee scrutinizes the expenditure of the different departments of the Government and reports to the House how far the public funds are utilized in accordance with the budgetary provisions. The Estimates Committee examines the working of the various ministries and suggests measures to ensure economy and improve efficiency. Select Committees are set up whenever the House feels that certain legislative measures need detailed study. The Committee on Privileges deals with cases referred to it relating to breach of privilege. The Rules Committee ensures that the rules for the conduct of the business of the House work smoothly and suggests amendments to them if necessary, while the Committee on Assurances takes steps to see that the promises made by ministers are carried out in a reasonable time.

The Rajya Sabha is the Upper House. It consists of not more than 250 members. Of these, twelve are nominated by the President from among those with special knowledge or of practical experience in literature, science, art and social service. The rest are chosen by the elected members of the Legislative Assemblies of States in accordance with the system of proportional representation by means of the single transferable vote. The Vice-President of the Indian Republic who is the ex-officio Chairman of the Rajya Sabha, presides over its meetings and in his absence, the Deputy Chairman, elected by the members from among themselves, takes the Chair.

The Rajya Sabha is never dissolved but one-third of its members retire every two years. A candidate for membership should be a citizen of India above thirty-five years of age. The Rajya Sabha can also control the Cabinet by means of questions, adjournment motions, and critical speeches, but it cannot remove the ministers by a vote of censure. It can initiate any bill except a money bill, and its consent is essential for other bills to become law.

However, if the Rajya Sabha declines within six months to pass a bill sent up by the Lok Sabha, it will become law as passed by the Lower House. The Rajya Sabha can also amend a money bill with the concurrence of the Lok Sabha. But if the Rajya Sabha does not give its assent to a money bill passed by the Lok Sabha within fourteen days of its reference to the Rajya Sabha, it will be deemed to have been passed in the form in which it was adopted by the Lower House.

Finally, we should refer to another important power vested in the Indian Parliament. Unlike many other federations, Parliament in India is empowered, under Article 3 of the Constitution, to form a new State by separation of territory from any State or uniting two or more States or parts of States or by uniting any territory to a part of any State; increase or decrease the area of any State; alter the boundaries of any State; and alter the name of any State. In bringing about these changes, the legislatures concerned have the right only to an expression of view on the proposals.

STATE GOVERNMENTS

So far as States are concerned, there are at present sixteen of them, namely, Andhra Pradesh, Assam, Bihar, Gujarat, Jammu and Kashmir, Kerala, Madhya Pradesh, Madras, Maharashtra, Mysore, Nagaland, Orissa, Punjab, Rajasthan, Uttar Pradesh and West Bengal.[1] It is important to note that many States are far bigger in area and population than some independent countries of Europe. For example, the Uttar Pradesh has an area of 1,13,654 square miles and a population of fifty-four million, Madhya Pradesh has 1,71,217 square miles and a population of thirty-two million and Andhra Pradesh has 1,06,286 square miles and a population of thirty-six million. The States enjoy a good deal of autonomy in the spheres allotted to them by the Constitution but, as pointed out earlier, in practice their powers have been to some extent whittled down on account of the exigencies of defence and development.

The executive power in the State is vested in the Governor. Unlike the USA where the State Governor is elected by the people, in India he is appointed by the President on the advice of the Union Cabinet. The Governor shall be a citizen of India, above thirty-five years and he shall not be a member of either House of Parliament or the State Legislature; nor shall he hold any other office of profit. He remains in office during the pleasure of the President and normally his tenure is five years.

The Governor is the Constitutional Head of the State. He is provided with a Council of Ministers, with the Chief Member at the head, to advise him in the exercise of his functions except where he is required by the Constitution to act in his discretion.[2] The leader of the majority party in the Lower House of the State Legislature is appointed as Chief Minister by the Governor, and the other ministers are appointed on the advice of the Chief Minister. The Chief Minister is enjoined to communicate to the Governor all decisions of the Council of Ministers relating to the administration of the affairs of the State and proposal of legislation; and to furnish such other information as the Governor may call for. The Governor may also submit for the consideration of

[1] In addition there are nine Union Territories, namely, Andaman and Nicobar Islands, Delhi, Himachal Pradesh, Laccadive Minicoy and Amindivi Islands, Manipur, Tripura, Dadra and Nagar Haveli, Goa, Daman and Diu and Pondicherry.
[2] But only in Assam the Governor is empowered to act in his discretion in regard to the administration of frontier areas. In other States, the Governors do not have to act in their discretion.

CABINET GOVERNMENT IN INDIA

the Cabinet any matter on which a decision has been taken by a Minister but which has not yet been considered by the Cabinet.

The Governor has certain legislative powers also. Laws passed by the Legislative become valid only after his assent. He is empowered to withhold his assent to a bill, to reserve it for the President's consideration or return the bill to the Legislature for reconsideration. The Governor also can issue Ordinances when the Legislature is not in session and immediate action is called for. He may address the Legislature either separately or jointly. He may send messages to the Legislature whether in respect of a bill pending before it or otherwise.

As regards financial powers, the Constitution provides that the Governor shall in respect of every financial year cause to be laid before the Legislature a statement of the estimated receipts and expenditure of the State for that year. No demand for a grant shall be made except on his recommendation.

The judicial powers of the Governor consist of the right to grant pardons, reprieves, respites or remissions of punishment to any person convicted of any offence against any law relating to a matter under the jurisdiction of the State Government.

Every State is provided with a Legislative Assembly. Some States have two Houses—the Legislative Assembly and Legislative Council.[1] The Assembly is more popular and powerful. Members of the Assembly are chosen by direct election on the basis of adult suffrage, but a certain number of seats is reserved for Scheduled castes and Scheduled tribes as well as for Anglo-Indians. Normally the duration of the Assembly is five years. The Assembly elects its own Speaker and Deputy Speaker. The strength of the Assembly shall not be more than 500 and not less than sixty.

The Legislative Council is a permanent body not subject to dissolution. One-third of its members retire every two years. The Constitution provides that the Council's strength shall not exceed one-fourth of the total number of members of the Legislative Assembly of the State, but in no case it shall be less than forty. Of the total number of members of the Council, (a) as

[1] The States with bicameral legislature are Bihar, Maharashtra, Madras Punjab, Uttar Pradesh, West Bengal, Andhra Pradesh, Mysore, Madhya Pradesh, and Jammu and Kashmir.

nearly as one-third is elected by municipalities, district boards and such other local bodies; (b) one-twelfth is to be elected by those who have been for at least three years graduates of an Indian university or its equivalent; (c) one-twelfth by persons who have been at least for three years engaged in teaching in schools not below the secondary standard; (d) one-third to be elected by the Assembly from among persons who are not members of the Assembly; and (e) the rest will be nominated by the Governor from among persons with special knowledge or practical experience in literature, science, art, the co-operative movement, and social service. Members are elected in accordance with the system of proportional representation with the single transferable vote.

The State Cabinets are collectively responsible to the Lower House of the Legislature. They remain in office so long as they enjoy its confidence. The Ministers are in charge of one or more departments and jointly they formulate the policy of the State Government. The Cabinet procedure in the States is more or less the same as at the Centre.[1] But the strength of the Cabinet varies from State to State.[2] In some States, in addition to Cabinet Ministers, there are Ministers of State and Deputy Ministers.

ZONAL COUNCILS

A number of States has been grouped together into zones under the States Reorganization Act of 1956. There are at present five zones—the Northern Zone with the Punjab, Rajasthan, Jammu and Kashmir, Delhi and Himachal Pradesh; the Central Zone with Uttar Pradesh and Madhya Pradesh; the Eastern Zone with Bihar, Orissa, West Bengal, Assam, Manipur and Tripura; the Western Zone with Gujarat, Maharashtra and Mysore, and the Southern Zone with Andhra Pradesh, Madras and Kerala.

The zonal council consists of a Minister of the Government of India nominated by the President, the Chief Minister of the State concerned and two ministers nominated by the State Governors. The Minister nominated by the President is the Chairman of the zonal council.

[1] This aspect has been dealt with in chapter IV.
[2] This has been discussed in detail in chapter IX.

The zonal councils have been formed to serve as a forum to bring about closer co-operation among the States, to settle inter-State disputes and to formulate inter-State development schemes. The councils take decisions by majority vote, the Chairman having a casting vote. Sometimes, two or more zonal councils may hold joint meetings. Each council has also a Secretariat to carry out its work.[1]

THE JUDICIARY

The Indian Constitution provides for a Supreme Court with a Chief Justice and a number of other judges, all of whom are appointed by the President. The Supreme Court has exclusive jurisdiction in disputes between the Government of India and the States and between the States themselves. The Court has appellate jurisdiction in civil and criminal cases and the power to sanction special leave to appeal from any judgment, decree or order passed by any court in the country. The Court also issues directives, orders or writs for the enforcement of Fundamental Rights. The law declared by the Supreme Court is binding on all courts in India. Besides, the Supreme Court may advise the President on such questions of law or fact as may be referred to it by him. Above all, the Court has the power to nullify the acts of Parliament and State Legislations on the ground that such laws violate the Constitution. Thus the Supreme Court plays a crucial role in Indian democracy by acting as the guardian of the Constitution and protector of the people's fundamental rights.

The judiciary in the States consists of a High Court and other subordinate courts. The High Court has a Chief Justice and other judges whose number is fixed from time to time by the President.

[1] In practice, the activity of the zonal councils depends largely on the personality of the Union Home Minister. As the *Statesman* of Calcutta remarked in an editorial in January 1965, 'The zonal councils, heralded with some fanfare, are kept longer in mothballs than out, and even when they are convened, are mostly called upon to deal with relatively minor matters. Pandit Pant, when Home Minister, took the councils seriously, and had interesting ideas about them. But these died with him. To Mr Shastri's temperament the councils were a gift; but if he used them to evolve a consensus on many problems the country did not hear about it. Mr Nanda has yet to show what his intentions are. So if Mr Kamaraj wishes to put the zonal idea to work, he has many precedents to ignore.'

The High Courts are the highest courts of appeal in civil and criminal matters in the States. The High Courts in Bombay, Madras and Calcutta have both original and appellate jurisdiction.

These then are the main features of the Indian Constitution. How it has been working in the last sixteen years will be evident from the manner in which the Central Cabinet has been carrying on the administration of the country.

CHAPTER IV

HOW THE CABINET WORKS

PRACTICE IN BRITAIN

A description of the essential aspects of the cabinet system, as it has developed in England and from whose Constitution we have incorporated its main features, will be helpful to the proper understanding of the working of the Indian Cabinet. Writers on the British Constitution have used expressive phrases to emphasize the importance of the Cabinet. Bagehot, for instance, calls it 'the hyphen that joins, the buckle that fastens, the executive and legislative departments together.' Sir John Mariott refers to it as 'the pivot round which the whole political machinery revolves.' In the words of Ramsay Muir, the Cabinet is 'the steering wheel of the ship of State,' while Sir Ivor Jennings considers it as 'the core of the British Constitution.'

The chief characteristics of the British Cabinet are political homogeneity, responsibility to the House of Commons, joint responsibility, and the ascendancy of the Prime Minister.

Political homogeneity means that members of the Cabinet should belong to the same party. Their outlook should be more or less similar and their loyalty to persons and principles should, to a great extent, be common. In a coalition cabinet there will be members from more than one party but this does not affect the principle of homogeneity so long as they agree to work on the basis of collective responsibility.

The members of the Cabinet are responsible to the House of Commons for 'every policy that they embark upon and for every action that they take.' In the early stages of the development of the cabinet system in England, ministerial responsibility was an individual, not a collective, matter. Ministers were often impeached individually and removed from office when the Sovereign declined to dismiss them.

But by the end of the eighteenth century, joint responsibility had become a well established practice in the British Constitution. This principle means, according to Lord Morley,

'that every important piece of departmental policy is taken to commit the entire Cabinet and its members stand or fall together. The Chancellor of the Exchequer may be driven from office by a bad despatch from the Foreign Office and an excellent Home Secretary may suffer for the blunders of a stupid Minister of War. The Cabinet is a unit—a unit as regards the Sovereign and a unit as regards the legislature. It gives its advice as a single whole both in the royal closet and in the hereditary or representative chamber . . . The first mark of the Cabinet, as that institution is now understood, is united and indivisible responsibility.'

Collective responsibility does not mean that a minister can misbehave with impunity. A minister can certainly be dismissed if he commits any act of official indiscretion. Or he may resign of his own accord when he knows that he has incurred the displeasure of the public and parliament, and that the latter will censure him.

The ascendancy of the Prime Minister is another fundamental feature of the Cabinet. For many years, the Prime Minister's position was not officially recognized. Walpole, Britain's first Prime Minister, was not only unwilling to be designated as such but denied any intention to assume supremacy in the Cabinet[1] and, strange as it may seem, it was only in 1937 that statutory recognition was given to this post. But the Prime Minister invariably has been holding a ministerial position, usually that of the first Lord of the Treasury. To what extent the Prime Minister is able to dominate the Cabinet depends largely on his own personality. As we have explained in a subsequent chapter, recent developments in the political and economic sphere have enormously enhanced the power and prestige of the office of the British Prime Minister.

The Cabinet is the chief executive body. In a parliamentary democracy, the executive consists broadly of two elements—the

[1] Walpole said: 'I unequivocally deny that I am sole Prime Minister and that to my influence and discretion all the affairs of Government must be attributed.'

political and the bureaucratic. The political element is represented by ministers and the bureaucratic element by civil servants. Ministers remain in office so long as they enjoy the confidence of the legislature. Ministerial changes do not normally affect civil servants. The latter enjoy permanency of tenure. Civil servants are experts while ministers generally are amateurs. The success of democracy depends chiefly on how closely and efficiently the expert and the amateur work together in the interests of the country.

The main functions of the Cabinet are to lay down policies, to initiate legislation and to co-ordinate the work of the various departments of the Government. It is the Cabinet's responsibility to control, direct and instruct the administration and to see that the will of the nation as expressed in parliament is carried out.[1]

PROCEDURE IN INDIA

Articles 74 and 75 of the Indian Constitution, quoted below, describe the functions of the Cabinet:

74 (1) There shall be a Council of Ministers with the Prime Minister at the head to aid and advise the President in the exercise of his functions.

(2) The question whether any and, if so, what advice was tendered by Ministers to the President shall not be enquired into in any court.

75 (1) The Prime Minister shall be appointed by the President, and other ministers shall be appointed by the President on the advice of the Prime Minister.

[1] The functions of the British Cabinet were described in the Report of the Machinery of Government Committee of 1918 as follows:
(1) The final determination of the policy to be submitted to Parliament;
(2) The supreme control of the national executive in accordance with the policy prescribed by Parliament;
(3) The continuous co-ordination and delimitation of the activities of the several departments of State.
But the above description does not fully and clearly bring out the important role of the British Cabinet of the present day. As Byrum E. Carter points out, 'one would not realize from the statement that the Cabinet actually exercises effective control over the Parliament and that nearly every measure of major importance is of Cabinet origin. . . . The theory of parliamentary control of the Cabinet is only an illusion behind which is hidden the reality of Cabinet control of the Parliament.' (*The Office of Prime Minister* by Byrum E. Carter.)

(2) The Ministers shall hold office during the pleasure of the President.

(3) The Council of Ministers shall be collectively responsible to the House of people.

(4) Before a minister enters upon his office, the President shall administer to him the oaths of office and of secrecy according to the forms set out for the purpose in the Third Schedule.

(5) A minister who, for any period of six consecutive months, is not a member of either House of Parliament shall, at the expiration of that period, cease to be a minister.

(6) The salaries and allowances of ministers shall be such as Parliament may from time to time determine and until Parliament so determines, shall be as specified in the Second Schedule.

The Indian Constitution does not use the word Cabinet but it does incorporate the essential features of the Cabinet system as it operates in Britain, such as the supremacy of the Prime Minister and collective responsibility. Although the Constitution says that the ministers shall hold office during the pleasure of the President, in practice they can do so only as long as they enjoy the confidence of the Prime Minister. However, there have been instances when a minister could not continue in office even when he had the confidence of the Prime Minister. The most conspicuous example was that of V. K. Krishna Menon who, as Minister for Defence, was forced to resign in November, 1962 by pressure of public opinion although the Prime Minister was very anxious to retain him in the Cabinet.[1]

The Indian Cabinet generally meets once in a week. The meetings are held in New Delhi at Rashtrapati Bhawan where the office of the Cabinet Secretariat is also situated. Sometimes, particularly when Parliament is in session, more than one meeting in a week may be held, depending on the urgency and importance of the business to be transacted. The agenda and the connected papers are circulated to the members of the Cabinet a few days prior to the meeting. An item not on the agenda can be raised at the meeting with the permission of the Prime Minister, provided it is of great urgency. The duration of a Cabinet meeting depends

[1] This is described in detail in chapter VI.

43

on the nature of the agenda. The longest session ever held by the Cabinet was on October 14, 1964 when it sat for four hours at a stretch to consider the outline of the fourth Five-Year Plan.

Only Cabinet Ministers are entitled to attend the meetings. But Ministers of State are asked to attend when the subjects with which they deal come up for discussion or when the Cabinet Minister concerned is unable to be present. Chief Ministers are sometimes invited to the meetings when questions relating to their States are discussed and their presence is considered helpful. For example, P. C. Sen, Chief Minister of West Bengal and B. Patnaik, Chief Minister of Orissa, attended the Cabinet meeting on June 6, 1963 when the food problem in the Eastern region was causing concern. When issues of a technical nature—economic, scientific or military—are discussed, the expert concerned is invited to the meeting and explain personally. The Deputy Chairman and the members of the Planning Commission are also asked to attend when problems relating to their respective planning portfolios are on the agenda.

The Prime Minister presides over the Cabinet meetings. In his absence, the Deputy Prime Minister used to preside so long as Sardar Patel held that post. Thereafter, the practice has been for the seniormost minister to take the Chair when the Prime Minister is unable to preside. Among those who have presided over the Cabinet meetings at one time or the other are Maulana Azad, Govind Ballab Pant, Morarji Desai and Gulzarilal Nanda.

There is no quorum for Cabinet meetings. A vote is taken rarely, the decisions being arrived at on the basis of mutual discussions and understanding. Referring to the practice in the British Cabinet, Attlee told his biographer Francis Williams: 'You don't take a vote. No, never. You might take it on something like whether you meet at 6.30 or 7.30 but not on anything major. In the same way, you never take a vote at a Commonwealth meeting of Prime Ministers. The Prime Minister collects the voices.' Herbert Morrison says: 'No voting, for the holding up of hands or the calling of Aye and No would not only be regarded as a breach of Cabinet decorum but would also be felt to symbolize and demonstrate, nakedly and unashamedly, a lack of Cabinet unity and solidarity, which is always deprecated.' In this respect also the Indian Cabinet is following the same procedure as in England.

The decisions taken at the Cabinet meetings are forwarded to the ministries concerned. The records of Cabinet meetings are kept confidential and in matters of exceptional secrecy, the decisions are not put down in writing.[1]

There are no definite rules as regards the subjects to be brought up for the Cabinet's decision. Matters of a routine nature are disposed of by the relevant department. Only very important issues are referred to the Cabinet. Sometimes even major problems are decided by the minister concerned in consultation with the Prime Minister or they are referred to the committee of the Cabinet and later confirmed by the latter. In some cases, the Prime Minister may take the decision on his own responsibility and then inform the Cabinet. Whether a subject is to be placed before the Cabinet or not depends mainly on the nature of the problem and the discretion of the minister. It is no easy task for a minister to take a decision in this regard because as Sir Ivor Jennings says, 'a minister who refers too much is weak, he who refers too little is dangerous.'

CABINET AND BUDGET

A matter of great importance that the Cabinet does not discuss is the general budget. It may seem odd indeed that such a vital subject as the budget, which affects intimately every department of the Government, should be outside the purview of the Cabinet. The detailed taxation proposals, prepared by the Finance Minister, are shown only to the Prime Minister and perhaps to one or two senior ministers. This procedure may appear unsatisfactory. In fact, Asok Chanda, former Comptroller and Auditor General of India, does not seem to favour the present practice of preparing the Central budget. He recalls in his book *Indian Administration* that till 1935 the Viceroy's Executive Council

[1] Despite their confidential nature, Cabinet decisions sometimes leak out to the Press. For instance, Inder Malhotra, Political Correspondent of the *Statesman*, wrote in his paper on December 25, 1964: 'During seventeen years of freedom, the Cabinet has found time to devote thought to external publicity precisely twice: first in 1948 and then exactly ten years later in 1958.'

used to meet at a special session to discuss the budget proposals. But since 1935 this procedure was discontinued with a view to preserving secrecy. The Finance Member of the Council, in preparing the budget, consulted only the Secretary of State for India, the Governor-General and the provincial governments in respect of those proposals that affected the latter's revenue. The taxation measures were conveyed to the Executive Council at a special meeting on budget day. Chanda says that the adoption of this procedure by the interim government led to 'serious differences' over Liaquat Ali Khan's budget proposals of 1947-8. Chanda observes: 'Despite this experience, the responsibility for the budget remains with the Finance Minister who discusses his taxation proposals with the Prime Minister and obtains his approval. The Prime Minister may take one or more of his senior colleagues into his confidence or direct the Finance Minister to do so; but the proposals are divulged to the Cabinet only on the budget day in Parliament as before. So much for joint responsibility in a vital matter affecting directly the economic life of the country and indirectly its political orientations.'

C. Rajagopalachari also strongly criticized the budget procedure while commenting on the budget of 1963-4 which imposed additional taxation of about Rs. 275 crores in a single year.

Rajagopalachari said:

'The way in which the budgets are made and got ready for presentation leaves no room for the whole or a material section of the Cabinet to examine and advise upon it, or even to go through it. In order to safeguard secrecy, all consultation is avoided. The budget is hatched by the officials working under the nominal guidance of the Finance Minister. If both the Prime Minister and the Finance Minister happen to be persons blissfully ignorant of the business of budget making, when all the economy of the country comes under the direct or indirect influence of the budget, the consequences are, what we see now, disastrous.'

But Chanda and Rajagopalachari do not seem fully justified in their criticism. It is very unlikely that Liaquat Ali Khan would have refrained from his drastic tax proposals if only members of the interim government had been made aware of the details before presenting the budget to the Central Legislature. Nor could Morarji Desai have avoided the heavy taxation in 1963-4 in view of the sharp and sudden increase in defence expenditure, following the Chinese invasion of India in October, 1962. It should be remembered that India is following in this respect the same practice in regard to the budget as prevails in England and other democratic countries. Lord Woolton stated in his *Memoirs*:

'The Chancellor is called upon to carry a responsibility much too heavy for any one man to carry ... Incidentally, other members of the Cabinet are placed in considerable difficulty by this problem, since they become politically committed to financial decisions with which they may not agree; the decision to resign, and so disturb all the other work of the Government, is a hard one to take unless some vital national principle is involved.'

In the view of Anthony Eden, 'A Chancellor of the Exchequer is wise if he shares his burdens to some extent with the Prime Minister; clearly, he cannot share them with the whole Cabinet.'

It should also be noted that though the Cabinet cannot discuss the budget before presentation, it can examine it afterwards, and it is always open to the Cabinet to modify the proposals before any mischief is done. Indeed, the Cabinet can even overthrow a budget altogether, in which case the Finance Minister will have to resign. The present procedure may not be perfect but so long as secrecy has to be maintained, there appears to be no alternative.[1]

[1] We may refer in this context to the embarrassing position in which the Minister for Industry found himself on February 29, 1964. In the forenoon of that day Nityananda Kanungo, Minister for Industry, told a member of the Lok Sabha, in reply to a question, that there was no proposal on the part of the Government of India to appoint a Commission to enquire into monopolies and concentration of wealth. But on the same day in the afternoon T. T. Krishnamachari, Finance Minister, while introducing his budget for 1964-5, announced the government's intention to set up a Commission to enquire into monopolies and concentration of wealth. A few days later when members of the Lok Sabha pointed out the contradiction in the statements, the Minister for Industry apologized to the House for the answer he had given on February 29, and explained that what was being considered by the Finance Minister would not be known to the members of the Cabinet. Kanungo added: 'At the time I gave the answer, the position stated by me was, as then known to me, correct and I have no hesitation in admitting this position.'

CABINET COMMITTEES

The Cabinet has a number of permanent committees to deal with important subjects like Foreign Affairs, Economic Affairs, Defence, Rehabilitation of Refugees, Parliamentary Affairs and so on. Sometimes committees are set up to consider special problems that may come up. Such committees are dissolved after their task is completed. For instance, in November, 1964 a special committee was constituted, consisting of the Home Minister, the Finance Minister, the Defence Minister, the Minister for Steel, the Law Minister, the Minister for External Affairs and the Education Minister to examine the charges of corruption levelled against the Chief Minister of Orissa and his colleagues. The duty of this committee was to recommend to the Prime Minister its views on the charges so as to enable him to decide whether a detailed enquiry was called for and if so, in what form it should be conducted. The committees may also set up sub-committees whenever necessary.

Referring to the role of Cabinet committees in England, J. P. Mackintosh says:

'No Government or Cabinet could operate nowadays without the shifting process and the preparatory work done by such committees. Sometimes committees set up to handle difficult and vital developments . . . take control of the major lines of policy and, for a period, become the effective centre of Government . . . Many issues are settled in these committees and never reach the Cabinet while some important questions go from the departments through the committees to the Prime Minister, the Cabinet receiving a report after a decision has been taken.'

This is practically the same procedure adopted in India.

In view of the great importance of Cabinet committees, it is understandable that ministers feel aggrieved when they are left out of some committee or the other. Thus Ambedkar complained to the Prime Minister when he was excluded from the Economic Affairs Committee in spite of the fact that he was primarily a student of economics and finance. In October 1962, the Emergency Committee was set up soon after the Chinese invasion, consisting of six members, namely Nehru, Krishna Menon, Morarji Desai, Krishnamachari, Lal Bahadur Shastri and Nanda. This committee assumed great importance and many issues were discussed and disposed of by it without reference to the Cabinet. The other twelve Cabinet Ministers felt hurt at their exclusion and three of them were reported to have protested to the Prime Minister against their being kept out of this committee. Their protest, of course, was unheeded because no Prime Minister in a democracy could be expected to consult all his Cabinet colleagues when the nation is confronted with a serious threat to its very existence, and vital decisions have to be arrived at quickly and implemented with speed and vigour. As Byrum E. Carter says, 'War requires that the Prime Minister exercise all his powers. It is not possible to rely upon brilliant colleagues, for decision will not wait for discussion nor will it wait for proposals to go through the regular channels.'

The formation of the Emergency Committee led to inactivity of most of the other Cabinet committees. The Economic Affairs Committee and the Foreign Affairs Committee, for instance, held no meetings at all throughout 1963. Early in 1964, an attempt was made to revive the regular Cabinet committees to enable ministers, who were not members of the Emergency Committee, to take part in decision-making.

THE CABINET SECRETARIAT

In England the Cabinet had no separate secretariat until Lloyd George introduced it in 1916 during the first world war. Till then, no record was kept of Cabinet meetings, apart from the report that the Prime Minister submitted to the Sovereign. In such circumstances, there was obviously a good deal of uncertainty and confusion about the decisions reached at the Cabinet meetings. As Lord Curzon remarked, 'The Cabinet often had the very haziest notion of what its decisions were: cases frequently arose when the matter was left so much in doubt that a minister went away and acted upon what he thought was a decision which subsequently turned out to be no decision at all, or was repudiated by his colleagues.'

In India the secretarial work of the Executive Council was

looked after by the Viceroy's Private Secretary. But until 1935 the Private Secretary was not allowed to attend the meetings of the Council. It was Lord Willingdon, Viceroy of India between 1931-36 who initiated the practice of taking his Private Secretary to the Council's meetings. Willingdon's successor continued this practice and the Private Secretary was also designated as the Secretary to the Executive Council. After the attainment of independence, the Cabinet replaced the Council, and the Council's Secretary was designated as the Cabinet Secretary.

Thus the Indian Cabinet from the very beginning has had the advantage of a separate secretariat. It consists of the main secretariat, Organization and Methods Division, Military Wing, Economic Wing and the Central Statistical Organization.

The functions of the main secretariat are to prepare the agenda for Cabinet meetings, in consultation with the Prime Minister; to circulate the agenda and the background papers to Cabinet Ministers and to record the proceedings of Cabinet meetings. The main secretariat also serves the Cabinet committees and sub-committees.

The Organization and Methods Division works directly under the Prime Minister and is responsible for constant and critical evolution of the administrative procedures with a view to improving efficiency. The Division has a Director who is also the Joint Secretary of the Home Ministry, a Deputy Director, an Assistant Director and secretarial staff. There are units of the Division in every ministry and meetings are held frequently to exchange ideas and evolve better methods of official procedures.

The Military Wing looks after the secretarial work of the Cabinet Defence Committee and of such other committees set up under the auspices of the Ministry of Defence. The Economic Wing serves the Economic Affairs Committee and other committees connected with problems of production and distribution.

The Central Statistical Organization set up in 1951 is responsible for co-ordinating the statistical work of the different ministries and for the publication of a number of periodicals such as the Annual Statistical Abstract, Monthly Abstract of Statistics, and the Weekly Bulletin of Statistics. The Central Statistical Organization works under the Honorary Statistical Adviser to the Cabinet.

We shall now consider the role of the Prime Minister in the Indian Cabinet.[1]

[1] Lal Bahadur Shastri, after he became Prime Minister in June 1964, introduced some changes in the cabinet procedure. These are described in chapter X. Cabinet procedure under Mrs Gandhi continues to be the same as it was under Shastri.

CHAPTER V

KEYSTONE OF CABINET ARCH

It was Lord Morley who described the Prime Minister as 'the keystone of the Cabinet arch.' He said:

'Although the Cabinet members stand on an equal footing, speak with an equal voice and, on rare occasions when a vote is taken, are counted on the principle of one man, one vote, yet the head of the Cabinet is *primus inter pares* and occupies a position of peculiar and exceptional authority.'

He added that the Prime Minister could assume powers not inferior to those of a dictator so long as he enjoyed the confidence of the House of Commons.[1]

The powers and functions of the Prime Ministers of England and India are to a great extent similar due to the fact that both countries have the parliamentary type of democracy. The Indian Prime Minister, like his counterpart in England, is the leader of the majority party in the Lower House of the Parliament. The Prime Ministers are formally appointed by the constitutional head of the state, namely, the Queen in England and the President of the Republic in India. The Prime Ministers remain in office so long as they enjoy the confidence of the Lower House. Their Cabinets are collectively responsible to it. In both countries the Prime Ministers select the ministers, allocate portfolios, co-ordinate work, settle differences, and help to impart harmony and homogeneity to the Cabinet. The Prime Ministers can compel recalcitrant colleagues to quit the Cabinet. In both

[1] J. S. Dugdale in his book *The British Constitution* says: 'From the point of view of political power, the phrase *primus inter pares* is unsatisfactory and ambiguous: if it means that all ministers including the Prime Minister are equal, then it is obviously wrong; but if it means that all ministers, except the Prime Minister, are equal it is nearer the truth.'

Peter G. Richards observes in his book *Patronage in British Government* that *primus inter pares* is 'a serious under-estimate of the Prime Minister's position'.

countries, the Prime Ministers have vast powers of patronage. But in India these are greater because the Prime Minister also appoints, subject to the formal approval of the President, the Governors of sixteen states. Moreover, by virtue of the unique position of the Congress Party, the Prime Minister has a major voice in the selection of Chief Ministers of states and their Cabinets.

In some important respects, however, the office of the British Prime Minister differs from that of the Indian Prime Minister. The British Prime Minister's powers and functions are based largely on constitutional conventions. In India, on the other hand, the role of the Prime Minister is described in the Constitution itself. The Prime Minister in Britain must be a member of the House of Commons, and he cannot take part in the discussions in the House of Lords. The Indian Constitution does not specifically prevent a member of the Rajya Sabha or the Upper House from becoming the Prime Minister; but by convention he will have to be an elected member of the Lok Sabha or the Lower House, since it is the more popular and representative chamber. But he can take part in the proceedings of the Rajya Sabha as well.[1] The British Prime Minister does not hold charge of any particular department; he confines himself to general supervision and overall control of the ministry. But in India, until recently, the Prime Minister, in addition to his duties of co-ordination and supervision, was in charge of the Ministry of Foreign Affairs. In both countries the office carries tremendous prestige. It calls for tact and talent of a high order, and it was fortunate that India chose as her first Prime Minister a leader of the ability and integrity of Jawaharlal Nehru.

Nehru became Prime Minister at fifty-eight, the average age at which many Prime Ministers of England assumed office in the present century. Asquith and Baldwin were both fifty-six, Salisbury fifty-five, Lloyd George fifty-three, Balfour fifty-four and Eden fifty-seven when they formed their first administration. But two of the famous Prime Ministers—Churchill and Attlee—could occupy 10 Downing Street, only when they were sixty-six and sixty-eight respectively.

[1] However, Mrs Gandhi was elected as Prime Minister in January 1966 although she was not a member of the Lok Sabha. See chapter XII.

Most Prime Ministers of England had acquired vast parliamentary or ministerial experience before they held this high office. For example, Henry Campbell-Bannerman has been a member of the House of Commons for thirty-eight years, Balfour for twenty-eight years, Asquith for twenty-two years, Lloyd George for twenty-six years, Baldwin for fifteen years, Mac-Donald for eighteen years, Churchill for forty years and Attlee for twenty years, prior to their first appointment as Prime Minister. But Nehru had no such experience. His father Motilal Nehru had won great renown for his debating skill in the Legislative Council of the United Provinces[1] and in the Indian Legislative Assembly where he was the leader of the Congress Party for many years. But Jawaharlal Nehru had no occasion to enter the legislature either at the Centre or in his State during the British regime.[2]

However, Nehru had other qualities and qualifications for being chosen as India's first Prime Minister. Educated at Harrow and Cambridge, he had travelled extensively in most parts of the world and acquired an intimate knowledge of international relations. He had achieved fame as the author of some best-selling books and his views on national and foreign problems were generally considered progressive. Although a student of science, he had taken, from an early age, a lively interest in economic and political problems. He recalls in his autobiography how while studying at Harrow, he surprised his teacher by reeling off the names of all the members of the Cabinet of Henry Campbell Bannerman who became Britain's Prime Minister in 1905, and he was the only student of his class who could do so. Moreover, by his sacrifice and suffering—he had spent a total of nine years in jail—he had endeared himself to millions of his countrymen especially the youth, who looked up to him for inspiration and guidance.

There were other leaders like Sardar Patel, Rajagopalachari

[1] Now called Uttar Pradesh.
[2] The only occasion when Jawaharlal Nehru came into contact with administrative problems, before he joined the interim government in September 1946, was in his capacity as Chairman of Allahabad Municipality. This experience to him was, in the words of Michael Brecher, 'highly instructive'. 'It brought the intellectual down to earth, into the realm of day-to-day administration with its many unsavoury features.'

and Rajendra Prasad who had also achieved all-India fame for their heroic part in the struggle for freedom and who, therefore, enjoyed in a considerable measure the affection and esteem of the masses. But the nation's choice fell on Nehru because, apart from his other qualifications, he was much younger than his colleagues; he was better known both in India and abroad than any other leader except Gandhi, and above all, he was preferred by the Father of the Nation for holding the most important office in independent India.

There were five Cabinets under Nehru's leadership. He formed his first Cabinet on August 15, 1947 and the second on January 26, 1950 when India proclaimed herself a Republic. The third, fourth and fifth Cabinets were formed on May 13, 1952 April 17, 1957 and May 12, 1962: after the first, second, and third general elections respectively. There were during the seventeen years of Nehru's rule many ministerial resignations and re-shuffling of portfolios, but the Cabinet as a whole maintained a remarkable stability and continuity mainly due to his personality and the overwhelming majority of the Congress Party in Parliament.

Nehru's career as Prime Minister can be divided broadly into three phases: the first, from August 15, 1947 till December 1950; the second from January 1951 till August 1963; and the third from September 1963 till his death in May 1964.

Phase I During the first phase, Nehru's authority as Prime Minister was severely limited due to the fact that the Cabinet consisted of several powerful colleagues who did not see eye to eye with him on major problems. There were veteran leaders who had not only not belonged to the Congress but who had been its staunch opponents. There was, for instance, Ambedkar, for many years a vehement critic of Gandhi and the Congress, especially in respect of their policy towards the untouchables. There was Shyama Prosad Mookherjee who was closely connected with a communal organization like the Hindu Mahasabha. There was Shanmukham Chetty who had been a pillar of the Justice Party which fiercely but unsuccessfully fought the Congress in South India. The Congress, nevertheless, included these leaders in the first Cabinet because of its understandable anxiety to make it as broadbased as possible and to create an impression among the masses that the Congress, though it had a huge majority in Parliament, did not want to monopolize power. It was eager to share it even with those who had opposed it all along during the British regime.

But it was not the presence of these men which really limited Nehru's supremacy in the Cabinet. It was Sardar Patel's powerful personality that prevented Nehru from having that amount of freedom in the Cabinet which he came to have after 1950. Although Sardar Patel throughout his career had been a staunch Congressman and a close follower of Gandhi, he and Nehru differed widely on many major issues.

Patel was a conservative in his views on political, economic and social problems. He never favoured a policy of appeasing the Muslims. He was, of course, eager to do justice to the Muslims but he was not, unlike Gandhi and Nehru, prepared to show them generosity at the cost of Hindus. He wanted to follow a tough policy towards Pakistan because he believed that any sign of weakness would expose India to attack and also lead to the oppression of the Hindu minority in that country.

In the economic sphere Patel wanted the country to achieve quick progress by enlisting the full co-operation and enthusiastic support of the business community. Consequently he did not approve of controls or other drastic measures like indiscriminate nationalization which would cripple private initiative and enterprise. The acute shortage of capital and technical skill was another factor that influenced Patel's policy. On land reforms, Patel's outlook was progressive but cautious. He insisted, as in the case of the Princes, that zamindars and jagirdars should be fairly compensated if their property was to be taken over by the Government.

Nehru, a firm believer in socialism, wanted the State to participate actively in the industrial development of the country. Although he acknowledged the importance of private enterprise, he would not give it the same amount of freedom that Patel favoured. Nehru was anxious to go ahead with sweeping agrarian reforms and he was impatient with legislative and judicial procedures that slowed down progress.

As Deputy Prime Minister and Minister for Home Affairs,

States, and Information and Broadcasting, Patel, fourteen years senior to Nehru in age, held effective control over the administration including police and propaganda; and his authority over the party organization also was very considerable. The administrative services appeared to have more confidence in Patel than in Nehru. The Indian Civil Service, which had produced some very able and patriotic officers, entertained genuine fears about their future on the eve of the transfer of power. They were afraid that their high salaries and privileges would be slashed and their security of tenure affected.[1] It was Patel who effectively dispelled their fears and inspired confidence in them by his assurance of fair treatment so long as they discharged their duties efficiently.

In view of Patel's strategic position, Nehru could not dominate the Cabinet in the same way as he could at a later stage. Although Nehru had a free hand in shaping foreign policy, in internal matters no major decision was, or could be, taken without the assent of Patel. There were occasions when Nehru and Patel were unable to agree on fundamental issues like the treatment of Muslims in India and the policy towards Pakistan. The details of their differences, which have been admirably described by Brecher in his biography of Nehru, need not concern us here. What is important to note is that at one stage the split became so serious that Nehru even considered dismissing Patel from the Cabinet while Patel, too, manoeuvred to get rid of Nehru. Fortunately, the intervention of Gandhi saved the situation. Gandhi declared straight out that the Prime Minister had a right to select his own colleagues and could ask Patel to quit if his attitude to Muslims violated Cabinet policy. Nehru and Patel also came to realize, particularly after the assassination of Gandhi, that they could not any longer afford to carry their differences too far and that unless they worked together, there could be no unity, peace, or progress in India.

[1] Nehru wrote in his autobiography: 'Of one thing, I am quite sure that no new order can be built up in India as long as the spirit of the I.C.S. pervades our administration and public services. That spirit of authoritarianism is the ally of imperialism and it cannot coexist with freedom. It will succeed in crushing freedom or will be swept away by itself. Only with one type of State it is likely to fit in and that is the fascist type. Therefore, it is essential that the I.C.S. and other services must disappear completely as such before we can start real work on a new order.'

From the country's point of view, it was certainly a great advantage that Nehru and Patel jointly guided the destinies of the nation in the period immediately after the attainment of freedom. Those were years of great anxiety and strain, and any false step would have seriously affected India's integrity and independence. Nehru and Patel acted as a check on each other, and their combined wisdom helped India to tide over a most critical phase in her history. As V. P. Menon, who played a crucial role in the transfer of power and in the integration of the States, says:

'It was, indeed, India's good fortune that during the initial stage of freedom, the destinies of the country were jointly entrusted to Pandit Nehru and Sardar Patel. One provided ideology while the other furnished realism. Both wielded equal hold on the Congress; as such, in every act of theirs, both Nehru and Patel were compelled to turn their searchlight inwards and think of the possible reaction to the other. This avoided the two extremes; and in politics, the middle course is always the safest. It is, in my opinion, the greatest tragedy that this combination should have lasted only for forty months after the transfer of power.'

Phase II Patel died in December 1950, and thereafter Nehru came to enjoy far greater power in the Cabinet than before. There was no one now with the same towering personality who could act as a check on him. There were indeed very competent and experienced leaders like Pandit Govind Ballabh Pant, Maulana Azad, Rafi Ahmed Kidwai, Gopalaswami Iyengar and, at a later stage, Lal Bahadur Shastri, Morarji Desai and S. K. Patil. But none of them could fill the void left by the indomitable Sardar. The designation of Deputy Prime Minister was specially created for him, and it is significant that till now this post has not been revived.

How then did Nehru utilize this tremendous power and responsibility? This question can be examined with reference to the choice of colleagues, allocation of portfolios and co-ordination of work.

Although in theory the Prime Minister in a democracy is free to choose his colleagues, in practice his freedom is greatly restricted by political and practical considerations. The Prime Minister must give due importance to leaders who have distinguished themselves by their patriotism and party work. A shrewd Prime Minister will always see that he gathers around himself colleagues who are not only able but whose exclusion may be a source of embarrassment.

As we have seen, in the early stages Nehru had to take into the Cabinet persons who had even fought against the Congress. His first Cabinet consisted of five non-Congressmen, namely, Shanmukham Chetty, John Mathai, C. H. Bhabha, S. P. Mukherjee and Ambedkar. But gradually the number of non-Congressmen was reduced, and by 1958 all the senior posts were held by Congressmen. In the choice of his colleagues Nehru had to take into account not only regional but also communal factors. Although all the States could not be given representation in the Cabinet, important ones like Uttar Pradesh, Maharashtra, Gujarat, Madras, the Punjab and West Bengal could not be unrepresented at any time. But Nehru gave too much weight to his own native State of Uttar Pradesh, which at one time had as many as four representatives in the Cabinet, including himself. Apart from regional claims, important communities like the Muslims and Sikhs must always be properly represented in the Cabinet. One unfortunate result of the influence of regional and communal factors was that the size of the Cabinet became big and unwieldy—an undesirable trend both from the point of view of efficiency and economy. This aspect has been discussed in detail in chapter IX.

So far as the distribution of portfolios is concerned, although this is mainly the responsibility of the Prime Minister, here, too, his freedom is limited by practical considerations. As Ivor Jennings rightly remarks, some members of the Cabinet choose themselves and they have much to say about their assignments. Consequently, the Prime Minister's free choice generally applies to less important offices.

In India, Sardar Patel was very keen in having the portfolios of Home and States. T. T. Krishnamachari declined to rejoin the Cabinet after the general election in April 1962 unless he was given Finance,[1] which he had held earlier. Manubhai Shah

[1] However, Krishnamachari joined the Cabinet in June 1962 as Minister for Economic Co-ordination. Later, in August 1963, he again became Finance Minister.

refused to take the oath as Minister of State for International Trade in April 1962 unless he was made a Cabinet minister. This was the first occasion when a minister refused to take the oath after his appointment had been announced by the President. But a few days later he agreed to work as Minister of State. Another example to show the Prime Minister's limitation in the choice of portfolios is provided by S. K. Patil's resistance to Nehru's attempt to shift his portfolio from Food to Railways in July 1963. Patil declared publicly that he would quit the Cabinet rather than change his portfolio and he submitted his resignation. Patil's objection was that a shift in his assignment, at a time when the Government was being strongly criticized for its failure to increase food production, would be tantamount to a reflection on his work. Nehru, therefore, dropped the proposal and allowed Patil to handle Food.[1]

Apart from limitations caused by personal factors, the distribution of portfolios in the Cabinet during the period under review was not done on a rational and realistic basis. Thus the Minister in charge of Food and Agriculture—a subject of great importance in view of the persistent food shortage—had no control over irrigation, on which depends largely the prosperity of agriculture, while the Ministry of Community Development, whose main task was to increase agricultural production, was handled by a separate ministry.

The Ministry of Commerce and Industry, another key portfolio, was split in the most haphazard way. This Ministry at one time was a compact one, controlling practically all the important industries and main aspects of industrial policy. But gradually many major industries like coal, fuel, oil, steel and heavy engineering were taken away from it and entrusted to separate Cabinet Ministers while International Trade was given to a Minister of State.

Defence, always a vital subject, became more so after the Chinese aggression in October 1962. Yet surprisingly there was considerable confusion even in this sphere. In 1962-63 there were two Cabinet Ministers dealing with defence—Chavan, the Defence Minister and Krishnamachari, the Minister for Economic

---

[1] But in August 1963 Nehru accepted Patil's resignation which was submitted under the Kamaraj Plan.

and Defence Co-ordination. Besides Biju Patnaik, the Chief Minister of Orissa, was also consulted on defence problems. In fact, Patnaik was given a room in the Ministry of External Affairs while he continued to be the Chief Minister of Orissa, until his resignation in August 1963 under the Kamaraj Plan.

There is perhaps nothing very wrong in allocating portfolios in the above manner, provided the Cabinet as a whole worked like a team and the Prime Minister effectively co-ordinated the work of his colleagues. But this was not done. On the other hand, the various departments pulled in different directions, ministers openly criticized one another, and no serious attempt was made to weld the Cabinet into a cohesive unit. And nowhere was this lack of co-ordination seen more glaringly than in handling the food problem.

Although under the Constitution agriculture is a State subject, the Central Government, too, has a great responsibility. It is the Centre's duty to regulate imports, to ensure adequate and timely supply of fertilizers, to sanction sufficient funds for agricultural schemes, and to arrange the smooth movement of foodgrains among the different parts of the country. But the Centre has failed to play its role properly. Brave declarations made by the Prime Minister from time to time to achieve self-sufficiency came to nothing, and even now, after over a decade of planning, agricultural production continues to be a gamble in rains and about Rs. 100/- to Rs. 150/- crores are spent annually on importing foodgrains from abroad. The way in which the Centre has handled the food problem provides an illuminating commentary on the working of the Cabinet system.

Ajit Prasad Jain, who was Minister of Food and Agriculture from December 1954 to August 1959, told the Lok Sabha after his resignation that important decisions on food policy were taken not by the Food Ministry or the Cabinet but by other agencies like the Planning Commission, the National Development Council and the Congress High Command and, regrettably, these decisions were often taken without a proper study of their implications. Referring, for instance, to the decision of the National Development Council to introduce State Trading in foodgrains and to increase the target for food production in the second plan from fifteen per cent to forty per cent, Jain said:

61

'On both the occasions, the decisions descended meteor-like from the sky. Neither specifically nor by implication was either of the items mentioned. No studies were made by the Ministry of Food and Agriculture which was responsible for implementing the decision. No notes were prepared and put up before the Council. No State Minister knew that he would be called upon to give his views until the proposals burst upon the Council.'

Jain also pointed out that complaints against the Food Ministry should be directed against other ministries—the Ministry of Irrigation and Power which was responsible for providing water for cultivators; the Ministry of Community Development for growing more food; the Ministry of Commerce and Industry for the supply of fertilizers; the Ministry of Health for checking the rise in population; the Ministry of Railways for movement of foodgrains, and lastly, the State Governments for the actual implementation of the various policies relating to agriculture.

S. K. Patil who succeeded Jain as Food Minister[1] also had to encounter serious difficulties on account of the lack of co-operation from other departments and from the Planning Commission. In fact, there were even open clashes between him and Nanda, the Planning Minister, on food policy. For instance, at the meeting of the All-India Congress Committee held in New Delhi in April 1963 Patil said that the Planning Commission had fixed unrealistic targets. He complained of lack of co-operation among the ministries and observed that his department had no control over Irrigation, Co-operation and Community Development. Nanda said that Patil's speech created the impression that the Ministry of Agriculture had nothing to do with agriculture but everybody else had! He called for clear ideas on the subject and said: 'Let not our own party man go on undermining our institutions.' Nanda confessed that many of the difficulties arose out of the fact that the administration was subordinated to politics and that one section of the Congress worked against another

[1] Patil was the fifth Minister to handle the Food Portfolio since independence. In December 1963, in a speech in Bombay, Patil expressed the view that frequent changes in the Food Ministry would not be helpful to solve the food problem. He added: 'It normally took a Minister about two years to acquaint himself with the complexities of the food problem. A Food Minister should be allowed about ten years before his ability to deal with the problem could be judged.'

even at ministerial level. 'If things were to improve,' he declared, 'there should be someone to enforce discipline'.

The lack of co-ordination was also seen in handling defence. We have stated earlier that after October 1962, defence problems were looked after by two Cabinet Ministers and a State Chief Minister. There is no doubt that the association of Patnaik with the work of defence was clearly unconstitutional and politically improper.

Patnaik was a young and daring politician—he was only forty-eight when he became Chief Minister of Orissa in 1962—and he had shown remarkable powers of organization in achieving the victory of the Congress Party in the elections of 1962. He took a keen interest in aviation and created a sensation when he flew the Indonesian Premier Sutan Shahriar during the Indonesian freedom fight against the Dutch. He was the first Indian pilot to land in Srinagar after Pakistan's invasion of Kashmir in 1947. He had also won his laurels as a successful industrialist. These achievements seemed to have impressed Nehru who described Patnaik as a man with 'unusual experience'.

But Patnaik soon proved himself tactless by the statements he made in the USA, which caused considerable embarrassment to the Prime Minister, the Defence Minister and Parliament. In March 1963 the Prime Minister sent him to the USA, with the approval of the Emergency Committee of the Cabinet, to have exploratory talks with the American government on certain aspects of defence. Ordinarily, either Chavan, the Defence Minister, or Krishnamachari, the Minister for Economic and Defence Co-ordination, should have been assigned to this job. But to the surprise of many, Patnaik was chosen; and in his talks with the US newsmen, he gave several details of India's military preparations and her requirements of radar, communication facilities, planes and other essential equipment.

Patnaik's disclosure caused indignation in India. Members of the Lok Sabha angrily asked the Prime Minister how Patnaik, the Chief Minister of a State, who was not a member of Parliament, could disclose vital facts about defence, which had been deliberately withheld from the House on grounds of security. Nehru admitted that he himself was 'surprised and distressed' but he sought to justify Patnaik's action by saying that the latter was adopting the practice followed in the USA where the authorities gave the public many particulars about military preparations. The Lok Sabha was however unconvinced and the Speaker deplored the fact that Patnaik had given out information that had been denied to the House.

The role of Krishnamachari as Minister of Economic and Defence Co-ordination created considerable uncertainty and embarrassment to his colleagues for some time. He rejoined the Cabinet in June 1962 as Minister without Portfolio but was designated Minister for Economic and Defence Co-ordination in November 1962. The main departments of this Ministry were the Department of Supply, the Department of Technical Development and the Department of Economic Co-ordination. None of these departments was new. The Supply Department was a part of the original Works, Housing, Supply and Rehabilitation Ministry. The Technical Wing was part of the Commerce and Industry Ministry, while there was already a cell in the Cabinet Secretariat dealing with the problem of Cabinet co-ordination. All these departments were now brought under one ministry.

But neither Parliament nor Krishnamachari himself was quite clear about the exact nature of his duties.[1] During the debate in Parliament on the budget in April 1963, members from all parties persistently questioned the Minister about his assignment and complained that, far from effecting co-ordination, the Ministry was creating complications.[2] Thereupon Krishnamachari explained that his Ministry's functions were similar to those of the Ministry of War Production in the United Kingdom, which was created in February 1942 and assigned to Lord Beaverbrook. The latter however resigned owing to ill-health and Oliver Lyttleton (later Lord Chandos) took it over. Krishnamachari read out the following passage from a speech delivered by Lyttleton in the House of Commons in March 1942:

[1] Krishnamachari described his portfolio as 'this nebulous assignment'. When Lord Mountbatten who visited India in June 1963 enquired of Krishnamachari about his work, he replied: 'My duties? That, my Lord, is what I myself would like to know.'

[2] Referring to newspaper reports of Parliament's criticism of his Ministry, Krishnamachari said: 'I read in a paper this morning that I have been under fire. Well, I did examine my coat today but I saw that no part of it had been singed.'

'I think it is the wish of the House that I should deal with the powers that have been conferred upon me. I would like to make it clear that they are the powers for which I ask, and that as far as I have been able to see during a short study of the problem, they are both adequate and precise. They have not been incorporated in a White Paper and I am sure the House will agree upon two things. The first is that to work upon a charter over such an extremely wide and varied field would be extremely difficult and would involve a very long document of almost legal precision when something more flexible is required. Secondly, I think that the actual control over certain vital supplies and services will count much more than any paper mandate.'

Krishnamachari added, 'That fits in with the broad picture of the duties that the Prime Minister has assigned to me.'

The division of responsibility for defence between the two ministers caused friction and misunderstanding. As the Parliamentary Correspondent of the *Statesman* pointed out in a despatch from New Delhi in April 1963,

'There is no evidence yet, there is much to the contrary, that the two ministers directly concerned with security are working together as a war-time team, each informed by a sense of crisis and each giving the other all the co-operation it can. In either of them one can hear loud complaints against the other, much of it backed by facts and figures, and each insists that greater efficiency is possible only if more powers are transferred to it.'

The lack of co-ordination was bad enough. What however was more unfortunate was that even senior ministers publicly criticized one another, sparing neither the Prime Minister nor the Government as a whole. We have already referred to the open quarrel between G. L. Nanda and S. K. Patil. Another example is that of Krishnamachari who, in his address to the thirty-fifth annual meeting of the Central Board of Irrigation and Power on February 25, 1963, criticized the Planning Commission (of which Nehru was the Chairman) for unrealistic planning, the Government departments for being too slow, the States for being too parochial, and his own Ministry of Economic and Defence Co-ordination for lacking the composite picture of production

C   65

plans which it should have. He also deplored the tendency to talk about the achievements of the various ministries through the Press and the radio, while what was more important was to realize the nature and extent of the work to be done.

Manubhai Shah, Minister of International Trade, wrote a personal letter to the Prime Minister in April 1963, strongly criticizing the working of the Ministry of Commerce and Industry, particularly its industrial licensing policy. He pointed out that the licensing policy was responsible for frustrating the socialistic objective of avoiding concentration of the means of production in fewer hands. The policy was also not helpful for promoting exports. He reiterated his views that his charge had been given a subordinate status in spite of the fact that it handled foreign trade; and he complained that a number of subjects relating to international trade did not come within his jurisdiction. For instance, light industries, certain heavy industries and free trade zones, which were intimately connected with the foreign trade programme, had been spread over three different ministries, as a result of which his initiative was considerably crippled.

Manubhai Shah was certainly within his right to draw the Prime Minister's attention to what he considered to be disabilities under which he was working. But his letter to the Prime Minister leaked out to the Press and provoked a debate in Parliament. Nehru denied that the Government's industrial policy was being implemented so as to encourage concentration of wealth. The details of Nehru's reply do not concern us here. What is significant is that a Minister of State should accuse the head of his own ministry of dereliction of duty and did not take care to keep his letter confidential.[1]

It is not surprising therefore that the Cabinet, lacking coordination, mutual understanding and team spirit, was unable to pull its weight in the country. The result was that efficiency in administration, at no time very conspicuous, deteriorated after the proclamation of the emergency. As B. M. Birla, the eminent industrialist, said in a speech in New Delhi in March 1963:

[1] When a member of the Lok Sabha asked Nehru how this letter had reached the Press, he replied that he had enquired into the matter and was satisfied that the leakage had not been caused by the Prime Minister's Secretariat.

'There is no sense of urgency, whether in peace-time or in war. We are told that everything should be done on a war footing. I am afraid I do not find any difference between war-footing and peace-footing; it is the same footing. The foot does not move, it remains stationary. Therefore, there is no progress.'

In the meantime, the economic condition of the people was steadily deteriorating. Production was on the decline and prices were going up. The steep increase in taxation on individuals and companies, introduced in the Central budget for 1963-4, created considerable discontent in the country. The imposition of the super-profits tax hit the companies hard while the compulsory deposit scheme caused resentment among the low-income groups. The gold control rules also resulted in acute distress among some sections of the population. All these factors, it was believed, were responsible for the rout of the Congress in the prestige by-elections held early in 1963 when three of its powerful opponents— Acharya Kripalani, Minoo Masani and Ram Manohar Lohia were elected to the Lok Sabha with thumping majorities. The electoral verdict produced a shock to the Congress and many of its leaders came to realize that the time had come to revise its policies radically and adopt bold and imaginative measures to strengthen its hold on the masses.

It was in this background that K. Kamaraj, the Chief Minister of Madras, formulated his proposal that top Congress leaders should quit office and take to party work. Actually it was not his idea in the beginning that there should be a mass resignation of ministers. The Congress in Madras had suffered some reverses in the by-elections and Kamaraj felt that he should give up office and devote more time to organizational matters. The idea somehow caught on and it was thought that the Congress, which had become complacent as a result of being in power continuously for too long a period, should show some dramatic gesture to convince the country that its leaders were not eager to stick to office for all time and that they were still inspired by the Gandhian ideals of sacrifice and service to the people. Accordingly, the All-India Congress Committee adopted in July 1963 the so-called Kamraj Plan by which all Congress ministers were required to submit their resignations to Nehru and he was entrusted with the responsibility for implementing it. Nehru alone was to decide who should remain in office and who should take up party work. Nehru also offered his resignation to the All-India Congress Committee but the latter promptly and firmly rejected it and reaffirmed its faith in his leadership.

Phase III Nehru availed himself of the opportunity to reorganize the Cabinet; and he accepted the resignations of six of his Cabinet colleagues; Morarji Desai, S. K. Patil, Lal Bahadur Shastri, Jagjivan Ram, Gopala Reddy and Shrimali.[1] The occasion was utilized to reduce the size of the Cabinet and to reallocate the portfolios in a more rational manner.[2] The important changes made were the following: Swaran Singh was made Minister of Agriculture and he was given overall charge of the Ministries of Irrigation and Power, and Community Development and Cooperation in respect of their activities connected with agricultural production.

With the transfer of Finance to T. T. Krishnamachari, the Ministry of Economic and Defence Coordination was abolished. But a Department of Coordination in the Ministry of Finance was created, the other departments in this Ministry being the Department of Economic Affairs, the Department of Expenditure and the Department of Revenue and the Department of Company Law.

A single Cabinet Minister was placed in charge of Education, Scientific Research and Cultural Affairs, the idea being to ensure the most effective utilization and training of the educated manpower resources of the country. M. C. Chagla, formerly Chief Justice of Bombay, Indian Ambassador in the USA, and High Commissioner in the UK, was given this portfolio.

The importance of the Ministry of Industry was restored to some extent by transferring to it control over cotton textiles, handlooms and jute which were managed by the Ministry of

[1] Nehru also accepted the resignations of six chief ministers of States, namely Kamaraj of Madras, B. Patnaik of Orissa, B. Jha of Bihar, B. A. Mandloi of Madhya Pradesh, G. P. Gupta of the U.P. and Bakshi Gulam Muhammad of Kashmir.

[2] The reallocation was done over a period of five months, from September 1963 to January 1964.

International Trade. Cement also was transferred to the Ministry of Industry from the Ministry of Heavy Industries.

Another major development was the appointment of Lal Bahadur Shastri as Minister without Portfolio. He was to perform such functions as might be assigned to him by the Prime Minister in relation to the Ministry of External Affairs, the Department of Atomic Energy, and the Cabinet Secretariat.[1]

The reallocation of portfolios[2] in the above manner was more rational than before. Nevertheless, there were some anomalous arrangements. For instance, subjects connected with industry and commerce, which were of crucial importance in a developing economy, came to be handled for four Ministers. C. Subramaniam was in charge of Steel, Mines and Heavy Engineering, and Humayun Kabir was given Petroleum and Chemicals, and both of them were members of the Cabinet. Manubhai Shah and Nityananda Kanungo, both Ministers of State, were given charge of International Trade and Industry respectively. Manubhai Shah was once again reported to have protested to the Prime Minister in January 1964 when cotton and jute textiles were taken away from him, pointing out that he could not promote exports effectively if he was not given control over these major earners of foreign exchange. His protest, however, was ignored.

The Cabinet during the third and last phase of Nehru's Premiership was more compact and homogeneous than ever before. Never since the achievement of independence had Nehru enjoyed so much power as he did since September 1963. He wielded absolute authority in the Cabinet and was in a position to implement his policies without opposition from his colleagues.

'He is now the apex not only of a highly centralized political machine but also an equally centralized and vastly more powerful administrative machine. In both these machines, loyalty has become the supreme virtue, and independence of thought a

[1] Shastri's recall to the Cabinet became necessary because of Nehru's illness. Nehru started delegating his functions to his colleagues only when ill-health made it impossible for him to carry on as before.

[2] It is interesting to note that ministers did not always confine themselves strictly to their respective portfolios. For instance, Chagla, the Minister for Education, argued the case for India in the United Nations on the Kashmir dispute in the early months of 1964. Similarly, Swaran Singh, the Minister of Food and Agriculture, actively helped the Prime Minister on certain occasions in handling external affairs.

dangerous adventure.' These words, used by R. H. S. Crossman to describe the present position of the British Prime Minister, seemed appropriate in the case of Nehru as well.

Nehru's role as Prime Minister has come in for criticism on several grounds. It is pointed out, for instance, that he sometimes took major decisions without consulting the Cabinet, that he was unable or unwilling to enforce discipline or ensure co-ordination, and that he deprived his colleagues of initiative by interfering too much with the details of administration. There is indeed a good deal of truth in these criticisms. But it is necessary to understand them in proper perspective.

It should be remembered that there is nothing unconstitutional if the Prime Minister on certain occasions first takes the decision and then gets it endorsed by the Cabinet. A study of the Cabinet system in other countries shows that nowhere is the Prime Minister able or willing to consult all his colleagues before taking every important decision.

Lloyd George and Churchill, it is well known, often took major decisions without consulting the Cabinet. So did Attlee in regard to the testing of the British atomic bomb and Anthony Eden in deciding to launch an attack on Port Said during the Suez Crisis of 1956. In these instances, the Prime Ministers concerned took into confidence only a few colleagues and permanent advisers. There have also been many similar examples in other countries. Indeed, R. H. S. Crossman goes so far as to say that 'a British Prime Minister is now entitled on really momentous decisions to act first, and then to face his Cabinet with the choice between collective obedience or the political wilderness.'

The lack of unity and team spirit in Nehru's Cabinet should not be exaggerated. The situation in this respect was far better in the final phase of his Premiership than in earlier years; and moreover, in no country has it been possible for the Prime Minister to eliminate entirely feelings of jealousy and misunder-standing among his colleagues.

Lord Beaverbrook, in his *Decline and Fall of Lloyd George*, recalls how Lord Curzon, the Foreign Secretary, had to face considerable embarrassment because his colleague Winston Churchill, the Colonial Secretary, often made policy statements regarding foreign affairs without consulting the Prime Minister or Curzon. 'Winston', said Lloyd George, the Prime Minister, 'has always been in the habit of making these pronouncements on his own. He did it under the Asquith administration constantly whenever there was a chance of a real limelight effect.'

Sir Hugh Dalton in his *Memoirs* observes: 'Politics, whether democratic or dictatorial, is a most competitive trade and I doubt if in any British Cabinet or its counterpart elsewhere, there has been no jealousy, no incompatibility of temperament, no sincere difference of opinion on grave issues.' The same point was also made by Krishnamachari when in April 1963, members of the Lok Sabha complained of serious differences between himself and the Defence Minister. Krishnamachari said: 'If two people do not have any differences all the time, one of them is useless. Many of the honourable members, who have levelled that accusation against me and my colleagues, are married people, and I am sure they have differences with their wives. Still they live together and work together.'

In the course of his long career as Prime Minister, Nehru sometimes made mistakes or took the wrong decisions but every time he was able to come out unscathed because of his tremendous prestige. Even when India was put to shame by the Chinese invasion in October 1962 and the entire country felt indignant about it, Nehru was spared although, constitutionally and morally, he was responsible for the failure to defend the nation against external aggression. On this occasion, the people's wrath was directed against Krishna Menon, the Defence Minister, and the pressure of public opinion forced him to quit the Cabinet. The incident affected Nehru's prestige to some extent but only for a short time and, as we have seen, after the Kamaraj Plan came into operation, he once again emerged as the nation's supreme leader, with more power and prestige than ever before.

Another important occasion when the Indian Prime Minister displayed lack of firmness and foresight was in regard to India's agreement with the United States over the loan of a transmitter. Soon after the Chinese invasion of India, the Government felt that it needed a powerful transmitter to counter effectively Chinese radio propaganda. Such a transmitter was readily available only from the USA. Accordingly, an agreement was signed between India and the USA by which the latter agreed to give a transmitter on loan to India on condition that the Voice of America would be permitted to broadcast through it for two hours every day. Another condition was that India should not use the transmitter for broadcasting to Pakistan.

But when the agreement was published, the Communist Party strongly protested against it, pointing out that a foreign country should not be permitted to broadcast from Indian soil. Moscow too was reported to be unhappy about it. Nehru, always sensitive to Russian reaction, quickly decided to back out of the agreement.

At the Press Conference in New Delhi on October 9, 1963, Nehru was closely questioned on this subject. His defence was: 'Mistakes occur even in the best regulated families.' He explained that the agreement was brought to his notice, in bits, on two or three occasions but not as a whole. He was, moreover, heavily occupied with other matters and did not clearly understand its implications. 'When the deal came to me as a whole,' said Nehru, 'and I saw it as such, I reacted strongly to it. Immediately afterwards, the next day or the day after, we were having a Cabinet meeting, and I put it before them and they also reacted against it.'

Another remarkable revelation made by the Prime Minister at this Press conference was that Gopala Reddy, the Cabinet Minister in charge of Information and Broadcasting, had 'nothing to do' with the agreement. When a correspondent asked him whether it was not strange that a minister should be unaware of what was happening in his own ministry, Nehru replied: 'It is not strange. The same criticism could apply to me. The External Affairs Ministry was also concerned with it very much.'

It is necessary to point out that there was nothing unusual about this agreement in the sense that similar agreements had been concluded by the USA with a number of countries like the UK, Greece, Liberia, Morocco, the Philippines and Ceylon. The UK also had set up transmitters in West Germany, Malaya and Singapore, with arrangements for the sharing of time as was provided for in the Indian agreement with the USA. Nevertheless, India went back on the agreement and, curiously, its repudiation evoked hardly any serious protest in the country, which was another proof of Nehru's remarkable hold over public opinion.

CHAPTER VI

REMARKABLE RESIGNATIONS

Ministerial resignations are a normal feature in a parliamentary democracy. Ministers may leave the Cabinet for many reasons— ill health, old age, or for taking up diplomatic or other assignments. They may also retire voluntarily owing to serious differences in policy, or may be compelled to go by pressure of adverse public opinion, or asked by the Prime Minister to quit for incompetence or for any other reason. In India there were many resignations from the Cabinet during the seventeen years of Nehru's regime, but here we are concerned only with those cases that involved important political and constitutional implications.

STANDARD OF INTEGRITY MUST BE ABSOLUTELY FIRST RATE

R. K. Shanmukham Chetty was the first minister to quit the Cabinet. As a young man, Chetty had taken an active part in the Congress but later he left it and joined the Justice Party of Madras. He had held a number of important posts under the British Government such as President of the Indian Legislative Assembly, Chairman of the Tariff Board and Dewan of Cochin, and he represented India at many international conferences. He had a profound knowledge of financial and economic problems, and just before the achievement of independence, the Federation of Indian Chambers of Commerce and Industry was contemplating whether to appoint him as its paid president. Few, therefore, expected that he would be offered the key portfolio of finance in India's first Cabinet. In fact, Chetty himself stated, when the appointment was announced, that he could not believe his eyes and that he was most happy.[1] But his happiness did not last long.

[1] We may recall Churchill's reaction to his appointment as Chancellor of the Exchequer, which came as a complete surprise to him. When in 1924, Baldwin told him, 'I can offer you the job of Chancellor', Churchill enquired, 'Of the Duchy of Lancaster?' (a sinecure post). Baldwin replied, 'No, of the Exchequer.'

Trouble arose soon when, while presenting his interim budget in August 1947, Chetty praised the generosity of the British in quitting India gracefully, but without saying a word about the part played by the Congress in winning freedom. This evoked protests from the Congress, and Chetty apologized to the party. His first budget presented on February 24, 1948 received warm appreciation both from the Congress and from other sections of Parliament. But unfortunately he seemed to have been rather tactless on withdrawing, against the advice from the Central Board of Revenue, certain cases from the purview of the Income Tax Evasion Commission. It was alleged that Chetty had grossly abused his authority by showing favouritism to his friends in the business community. The Cabinet considered the matter at two meetings and came to the conclusion that Chetty had done no wrong, and all that could be said against him was that he had committed an error of judgment. But the Congress Party was not convinced, and influential members like Pattabhi Sitaramayya and Anantasayanam Ayyangar vigorously asserted that Chetty had brought down the prestige of the Congress Party. Chetty, therefore submitted his resignation on August 15, 1948, exactly one year after he assumed office.

In his statement to Parliament, Chetty explained in detail the circumstances leading to his resignation and pointed out that the Prime Minister was 'good enough and generous enough to repeat on more than one occasion that he was thoroughly satisfied with my honesty and bonafides.'

'But,' he added, 'notwithstanding this assurance from the Prime Minister, I felt that in the context of the new independence that our country has obtained, in the context of the parliamentary institutions which we have begun to work, we must set absolutely the highest standards of integrity in public, not even the second rate standards would be sufficient for us. They must be absolutely first rate. Even though a minister's conduct and bonafides may be justified by argument, yet if, in the minds of our people, who may not understand these technicalities, there is room even for suspicions, such a minister ought not to continue in office, and it is under these circumstances that I requested the Prime Minister to relieve me of my office.'

POLICY TOWARDS PAKISTAN—WEAK, HALTING, INCONSISTENT

The next important resignations were those of Shyama Prasad Mukherjee (Minister of Industry and Supply) and K. C. Neogy, Minister of Commerce. They resigned because of their disagreement over the pact which Nehru had concluded with Liaquat Ali Khan, the Prime Minister of Pakistan, regarding the treatment of minorities in that country. The pact was strongly condemned particularly by Mukherjee in the statement he made in the Lok Sabha on April 19, 1950. 'My differences,' said Mukherjee who had served in the Cabinet for two-and-a-half years, 'are fundamental, and it is not fair or honourable for me to be a member of the Government whose policies I cannot approve of. I have never felt happy about our attitude towards Pakistan. It has been weak, halting and inconsistent.'

Mukherjee gave seven main reasons for his inability to accept the Nehru-Liaquat pact. In the first place, he said, two such agreements had been concluded before between India and Pakistan, and they had been violated by the latter. He felt that any agreement which had no sanction would offer no solution. Secondly, the crux of the problem was Pakistan's concept of an Islamic State and the ultra communal administration based upon it. The agreement side-tracked this cardinal issue. Thirdly, the agreement made it appear that India and Pakistan were equally guilty though clearly Pakistan was the aggressor. The provision in the agreement that neither side would encourage encitement to war sounded farcical so long as Pakistan's troops occupied a portion of Indian territory in Kashmir and warlike preparations were being conducted. Fourthly, the agreement made no provision to compensate those who had suffered, nor would the guilty ever be punished because no one would ever dare to give evidence before a Pakistani court. Sixthly, while Hindus would continue to come away from Pakistan, those who had come would not be prepared to go back. On the other hand, Muslims who had gone away could now return; and because of India's determination to implement the agreement, Muslims would not leave India. In such a situation, the Indian economy would be put to great strain. Finally, the agreement had reopened the problem of the

Muslim minority in India, thereby reviving those disruptive forces which were responsible for the creation of Pakistan.

In conclusion, Mukherjee appealed to those who had faith in the agreement to discharge their responsibility by going to East Bengal, not alone but accompanied by their wives, sisters and daughters, and bravely share their burden of joint living with the unfortunate Hindu minorities of East Bengal.

A PARALLEL AUTHORITY TO CABINET

The resignation of John Mathai from the Cabinet in 1950 was also due to fundamental differences. He started his career as a Professor of Economics in Madras and held a number of important posts under the British Government, such as Director-General of Commercial Intelligence and Statistics, and Chairman of the Tariff Board. After retirement from government service, he joined the house of Tata as a Director. He was given the Education portfolio in the interim government and he took over Finance on the resignation of Shankukham Chetty.

Mathai's resignation from the Cabinet was mainly over the appointment of the Planning Commission. Mathai himself was a believer in the need for economic planning and he was a signatory to the famous Bombay Plan of 1944, which was jointly put forward by a number of eminent industrialists including G. D. Birla and J. R. D. Tata. Mathai, however, felt that the proposed Planning Commission was unnecessary and unworkable.

In a statement issued on June 3, 1950, Mathai said:

'There are at present on the shelves of the various ministries of the Government of India plans costing nearly Rs. 3,000 crores, which have been held up for lack of finance, materials, and technical personnel. In my opinion, what is required at present is first to draw up a strict order of priority for the existing plans based on the available resources of the country and, secondly, to work out the existing plans in detail at the technical end because no blue-print can be put into execution until the technical issues have been worked out in detail.'

Mathai felt that new plans could be carried out only by

larger deficits which were 'unthinkable in the present circum-stances.' He was afraid that the Commission was tending to become a super-Cabinet, increasing the area of argumentation and discussion inside the government and causing delay in arriving at decisions on immediate problems. 'Cabinet responsi-bility has definitely weakened since the establishment of the Planning Commission,' declared Mathai. 'The members of the Commission,' he added, 'have been given the same place in the warrant of precedence as Cabinet ministers, and their salaries and allowances have also been fixed in accordance with those of Cabinet ministers. With the Prime Minister presiding over such a body, it is difficult to resist the Planning Commission develop-ing into a parallel authority of equal standing with the Cabinet.'

Mathai particularly objected to the arrangement by which a Cabinet Minister, holding the key portfolio of finance, was to serve as an ordinary member of a body of which the working head, namely, the Deputy Chairman, was a paid employee of the Government. He felt that this would weaken the authority of the Finance Minister and also that of the Cabinet.

Apart from his disagreement over the Planning Commission, Mathai complained that he was not getting the necessary co-operation from the Prime Minister and other colleagues in en-forcing economy in expenditure. The Standing Finance Com-mittee was the most effective safeguard against extravagance in expenditure and its approval was necessary for new proposals for expenditure even though they had been provided for in the budget. But he found there was a general tendency among min-isters to disregard the authority of the Standing Finance Com-mittee, some of the greatest offenders in this respect being the ministers working under the immediate control of the Prime Minister.

For example, the Standing Finance Committee had agreed to the proposal that India's High Commissioner in the United Kingdom should also act as the High Commissioner for Ireland, but no expenditure should be incurred for this purpose except his travelling expenses. But the then High Commissioner in the United Kingdom, V. K. Krishna Menon did not agree. So the matter was referred to the Cabinet, which decided that the Indian Embassy at Dublin should be provided with a building and staff. Mathai felt that when departures of this kind were approved by the Prime Minister, they had a demoralizing effect on other departments and caused no small embarrassment to the Finance Minister.

Another important point on which Mathai had differences with Nehru was the Indo-Pakistan Pact over which Shyama Prasad Mukherjee and K. C. Neogy had resigned in April 1950. Matthai had entertained grave misgivings about the pact; nevertheless, he agreed to give it a fair trial; and in the statement on his resignation he emphasized that 'under the guise of appeasement it was extremely important that we should be careful not to barter away with vital national interests.'

LAW PORTFOLIO—AN EMPTY SOAP BOX GOOD ONLY FOR OLD LAWYERS TO PLAY WITH

Ambedkar's resignation from the Cabinet was unique in many respects. Although the immediate cause was the delay in passing the Hindu Code Bill, he had strong differences with the Cabinet on other domestic matters as well as of India's foreign policy. In the statement on his resignation he vigorously attacked the Government for delaying the passage of the Hindu Code Bill, for pursuing a policy of discrimination against the untouchables, for adopting a policy of friendship with China, for alienating friendly countries in the world, and finally, for the manner in which Nehru was conducting himself as Prime Minister in utter disregard of well-established Cabinet principles. Ambedkar, in fact, walked out of the Lok Sabha on October 11, 1951 as a protest against the Speaker's refusal to permit him to make a statement on his resignation at the time he wanted.

As in the case of Shanmukham Chetty, the appointment of Ambedkar to the Cabinet came as a surprise both to himself and to the country. He had served for some time as a member of the Viceroy's Executive Council under British rule and had been a consistent critic of the Congress. He was not, however, happy with the Law portfolio given to him by Nehru because he knew, from his experience as a member of the Viceroy's Executive Council, that it was administratively of no importance, and that it gave him no opportunity to shape the Government's policy.

He described it as 'an empty soap box good only for old lawyers to play with.' He therefore told the Prime Minister that in addition to Law he would like to have some administrative portfolio. Nehru, it appeared, agreed to consider his request favourably, but nothing was done in this direction during the four years he remained in the Cabinet. 'Many ministers,' complained Ambedkar in the statement on his resignation, 'have been given two or three portfolios so that they have been overburdened. Others like me have been wanting more work. I have not been considered even for holding a portfolio temporarily when a minister-in-charge has gone abroad for a few days.'

'It is difficult to understand,' added Ambedkar, 'the principle underlying the distribution of government work among ministers, which the Prime Minister follows. Is it capacity? Is it trust? Is it friendship? Is it pliability? I was not even appointed to be a member of the main committees of the Cabinet such as the Foreign Affairs Committee or the Defence Committee.'

Among his other grievances was the treatment meted out to the Scheduled castes for whose uplift he had laboured hard for many years. He still found 'the same old tyranny, the same old oppression, the same old discrimination which existed before.' In contrast, the Muslims were well looked after and the Prime Minister's 'whole time and attention' was devoted to their protection.

In regard to foreign policy, Ambedkar felt that it lacked realism because it had left India practically friendless in the world. He expressed his 'deep dissatisfaction' about India's attitude to Pakistan. The condition of Indians in East Bengal was becoming intolerable but 'we have been staking our all on the Kashmir issue.' He was of opinion that the right solution to Kashmir was to partition it.

But the matter which actually led to his resignation was the treatment accorded to the Hindu Code Bill. Its passage had been delayed by about four years and the Cabinet ultimately decided that it should be got through in the winter session of Parliament in 1951. But subsequently the Prime Minister suggested that as adequate time might not be available for Parliament to consider the entire Bill, the marriage and divorce part of it might be enacted into law at that session. However, after a few days' discussion, the Prime Minister decided to drop the whole Bill including the marriage and divorce portion. 'This,' said Ambedkar, 'came to me as a great shock—a bolt from the blue. I was stunned and could not say anything. I was not prepared for the dropping of the Bill because others more powerful in the Cabinet wanted precedence for their Bills.' Ambedkar strongly criticized the conduct of the Minister of Parliamentary Affairs for his unhelpful attitude and dilatory tactics, and described him as 'the deadliest opponent of the Code.'

LABOUR MINISTRY ALMOST SUPERFLUOUS

Another important resignation on policy matters was that of V. V. Giri in February 1954. A prominent labour leader, he joined the Union Cabinet as Minister for Labour in May 1952. But he soon found that he could not see eye to eye with his colleagues on major issues. The first occasion when he met with serious opposition was in connection with the Industrial Relations Bill. The Ministers of Finance, Defence and Railways felt that the industrial establishments under them should be excluded from the purview of this Bill. Giri did not agree. Although the intervention and tactful handling of the situation by the Prime Minister brought about a compromise, Giri did not feel happy. He found that there 'was a growing feeling among the employing ministries that each could have its own way and its own policy, thus rendering the Labour Ministry almost superfluous in shaping Government's policy in this behalf.'

But the real cause for his resignation was the action of the Cabinet in modifying the Bank Award 1954 in such a way as to affect adversely the interests of bank employees. He felt strongly that the awards of tribunals should not be set aside by executive action except on rare occasions and for very weighty reasons. 'I am of the opinion,' he wrote to the Prime Minister on August 30, 1954

'that the Central Government should not have set aside the award in the manner it has done when it was the outcome of six years of careful consideration by three tribunals of the highest status. I hold the view that the sanctity of judicial awards must be honoured and respected in spite of the provision in the law permitting the contrary, and it is my firm conviction that Government should not exercise the legal power vested in it and unless and until it is established that the award in question, when enforced, will have consequences so grave as to upset the economy and stability of the country.'

He suggested that since the life of the award was only for one year, it should be accepted and enforced, and in the meantime, the Government should appoint a high-power commission to study carefully the full implications of the award. But the Cabinet did not agree. Giri, therefore, tendered his resignation.

FINANCE MINISTER'S RESIGNATION HAD NOTHING TO DO WITH FINANCE

The resignation of Chintaman Deshmukh had many unusual aspects. While his predecessors in the Finance Ministry had resigned for reasons connected with their portfolios, Deshmukh left the Cabinet on account of differences with the Prime Minister over matters which had nothing to do with finance. The main cause of his resignation was the decision of the Cabinet to keep Bombay as a centrally administered city for a period of five years.

Like Shanmukham Chetty, Deshmukh also came into the Cabinet with an expert knowledge of finance. A distinguished member of the Indian Civil Service, he had held important posts under the British Government. He was also connected with the Reserve Bank for about ten years, first as a liaison officer and then as Governor. After his retirement from the Bank early in 1949 Deshmukh acted for some time as India's Financial Representative both in Europe and in America and as Governor for India on the International Monetary Fund and the World Bank. He also accompanied Nehru as financial adviser on some of his European tours. In May 1950 on the resignation of John Mathai, he joined the Cabinet as Finance Minister after 'repeated requests' by Nehru. But in accepting the post, he warned the Prime Minister that he (Deshmukh) was 'apt to prove difficult where principles were involved' and that he would have to resign if there was a major disagreement. 'In that event,' Nehru told him, 'it would not be a case of your walking out alone.'

During his tenure as Finance Minister, Deshmukh had sometimes differences with his colleagues in the Cabinet over certain financial matters but these, not being of a major nature, were settled by mutual adjustment. What actually led to his resignation was the decision of the Government regarding the status of Bombay city and the manner in which it was arrived at.

The people of Maharashtra had strongly opposed the recommendation of the States Reorganization Commission to form a bilingual Bombay consisting of the whole of Maharashtra, including Bombay city, and Gujarat. The Government then announced their decision to keep Bombay city under Central administration. The people of Maharashtra did not agree and riots took place in Bombay towards the end of 1955 and the beginning of 1956 when, as a result of police firing, eighty were killed and 450 injured. Deshmukh pressed for a judicial enquiry into the Bombay firing but this was not conceded. In the meantime in June 1956, Nehru declared at a public meeting in Bombay that Bombay city would be administered by the Centre for a five-year period, and thereafter a final decision would be taken in a calmer atmosphere.

Deshmukh objected to the decision. His view had been that if the bigger bilingual Bombay State was not possible, there should be a separate Gujarat State and a separate Maharashtra State including the city of Bombay. He felt that the separation of Bombay city from Maharashtra would be a 'grave economic and political blunder, besides being unjust to Maharashtra.' He was particularly hurt by the manner in which the Prime Minister announced the decision without consulting the Cabinet.

As he said in the Lok Sabha in the statement on his resignation,

'there was no consideration of the proposal in the Cabinet or even by circulation. There was no individual consultation with members of the Cabinet known to be specially interested, as for instance, myself. There is no record even of a meeting of the committee of the Cabinet, and to this day no authoritative text of the so-called decision is available to the members of the Cabinet.

This instance is typical of the cavalier and unconstitutional manner in which decisions have been taken and announced on behalf of the Cabinet by certain unauthorized members of the Cabinet, including the Prime Minister, in matters concerning the re-organization of States.'

Deshmukh's statement caused some embarrassment to Nehru because a public reference had been made to the proceedings of the Cabinet. The Prime Minister denied in the Lok Sabha that the Cabinet had been kept in the dark about the various aspects of the Bombay issue. He said that the account given by Deshmukh was not quite correct in all particulars and that it was likely to give a wrong impression of what had actually happened. He pointed out that the matter was discussed in the Cabinet on many occasions and when a special committee was formed, the Cabinet was kept informed of its work. The Prime Minister added that Deshmukh by making his statement had been unjust to the several respected and senior colleagues of the Cabinet. Replying to the charge that the Prime Minister had been making statements without consulting the Cabinet, Nehru said,

'I am the Prime Minister of India. I know something of democratic procedure, about the Prime Minister's duties, the Constitution of India and the Constitution of Britain. The Prime Minister is the lynch-pin of the Government and he can make any statement on behalf of the Government.'

FINANCE MINISTER CAN FUNCTION ONLY FROM POSITION OF STRENGTH

T. T. Krishnamachari was the fourth Finance Minister to quit the Cabinet. As a successful businessman and as a legislator first in Madras and later in the Centre, he had won a reputation for hard work and deep knowledge of economic problems.[1] He joined the Union Cabinet in May 1952 as Minister for Commerce and Industry. But he submitted his resignation in June 1956 as a protest against the Cabinet's decision to reject Birla's proposal

[1] After he rejoined the Cabinet in 1962 Krishnamachari donated his entire private library, consisting of about 5,000 books, to a college in Madras.

to set up a steel plant in the private sector. Krishnamachari felt that in view of the acute shortage of capital and technical skill in the country, it would be wrong to prevent the private sector from erecting a steel plant merely on ideological grounds. But Nehru, who had just then returned from a tour of China, greatly impressed by her achievements, did not agree. He also did not accept Krishnamachari's suggestion to wind up the Production Ministry. Krishnamachari, therefore, tendered his resignation, but on the Prime Minister's persuasion, consented to continue in the Cabinet. He was then made Minister for Iron and Steel. The Ministry of Production was bifurcated and it was made responsible only for projects in the public sector, those in the private sector being left to the charge of the Ministry of Commerce and Industry.

Krishnamachari took over the Finance portfolio in July 1956 on the resignation of Deshmukh; and in this capacity he displayed considerable vigour and originality. In his budget presented in May 1957 he introduced three entirely new taxes—the wealth tax, the expenditure tax and the gift tax. Although the taxes proved unpopular with the business community, he was praised for his boldness in tapping new resources of revenue. But Krishnamachari could not remain long in the Finance Ministry because of the manner in which he handled the Mundhra Affair.

Haridas Mundhra, a young and ambitious businessman of Calcutta, had built up a vast industrial empire. His meteoric rise into eminence evoked admiration and jealousy, and suspicions were aroused about the methods adopted by him to acquire control over giant companies in quick succession. In 1956 the Life Insurance Corporation of India, a nationalized body under the control of the Finance Ministry, bought shares worth several lakhs of rupees in certain concerns of Mundhra. The transaction did not attract public attention for some time. But in December 1957 it was raised in the Lok Sabha, and several members persisted in holding an independent and impartial enquiry into the whole matter. It was argued that the investment of such large sums of public money in companies whose financial condition and prospects were far from satisfactory, was wholly unjustified. It was suggested that the shares were purchased by the Life Insurance Corporation with a view to helping the speculative activities of Mundhra. Allegations of corruption were also made. The Finance Minister's attempt to justify the investment on the ground that it was needed to support sentiment in the Calcutta Stock Exchange was considered unconvincing. Public indignation was aroused and so the Government agreed to conduct a judicial enquiry into the transaction.

M. C. Chagla, Chief Justice of the Bombay High Court, conducted the enquiry and his verdict went against Krishnamachari. There was, of course, no charge of corruption against him but he was criticized for an error of judgment since as Finance Minister the Life Insurance Corporation was under his jurisdiction. Chagla held that it was improbable that H. M. Patel, the Principal Secretary to the Finance Ministry, would have put through an unusual deal of this character without ministerial concurrence. The fact that the transaction was not repudiated by the minister seemed to indicate the latter's prior concurrence or subsequent acquiescence. Chagla said, 'The Minister must take full responsibility for the acts of his subordinates. He cannot be permitted to say that his subordinates did not reflect his policy or acted contrary to his wishes or directions.'

In a lengthy statement in the Lok Sabha on February 18, 1958, Krishnamachari explained the background to the L.I.C.'s deal with the Mundhra concerns, and pointed out that he had been unaware of its details for a long time until the matter was raised in Parliament. He suggested that something must have gone wrong in the Principal Secretary's appreciation of the Government's policy. As regards the constitutional position, Krishnamachari recalled that some years earlier certain senior Civil Servants attached to the Food Ministry had been actually prosecuted for corruption, but the Minister of Food was not called upon to submit his resignation. Krishnamachari felt that in his own case resignation was not called for; nevertheless, he wanted to go because he thought he would not be able to function effectively in the prevailing circumstances. 'A Finance Minister,' he said, 'can function adequately only from a position of strength and not from one of weakness.'[1]

[1] T. T. Krishnamachari again became Finance Minister in August 1963 but had to resign in December 1965 because he could not function from a position of strength. This is explained in chapter XI.

NOT EVEN NEHRU COULD SAVE HIM

The remarkable thing about V. K. Krishna Menon's resignation was that for the first time a senior minister was compelled to quit in spite of the vigorous and persistent efforts made by the Prime Minister to retain him in the Cabinet.

A close friend and colleague of Nehru for many years, Menon had worked as Secretary of the India League in London before the attainment of independence. Nehru chose him as India's first High Commissioner in the United Kingdom, a post which he held for about five years (1947-52). But his work in this capacity came in for considerable criticism for his failure to exercise proper vigilance in financial matters. The High Commissioner is responsible for the purchase of stores on behalf of India and Menon appeared to have shown slackness on certain occasions particularly in connection with the purchase of jeeps for the Indian Army. As a result, the Government of India was put to heavy loss. Nehru wanted to bring Menon into the Cabinet after the latter had relinquished his assignment in London. But the Prime Minister had to wait until public opinion, which had been critical of Menon's record as High Commissioner, became favourable. Moreover, not all of Nehru's colleagues were enthusiastic about his proposal to bring Menon into the Cabinet. Some of them feared that Menon, with his great influence over the Prime Minister, would be able to dominate the Cabinet—a prospect which they did not like in view of his well-known leanings to the Left. This, for instance, is what Maulana Abul Kalam Azad says in his autobiography about Menon:

'Krishna Menon professed great admiration for Jawaharlal and I knew Jawaharlal often listened to his advice. I did not feel happy about this, as I felt that Krishna Menon often gave him wrong advice. Sardar Patel and I did not always see eye to eye but we were agreed in our judgment about him.'

Menon joined the Cabinet as Minister without Portfolio. When about a year later he took over Defence, many were surprised that a key portfolio had been given to one who was reported to hold pro-Communist views. But Nehru had full confidence in him and gave him a free hand in organizing the vital department. Menon did some good work especially in stepping up the production of military equipment which was mostly being imported from abroad. But at the same time, he was accused by his opponents of perpetuating waste and extravagance in the Defence Ministry and, what was more serious, of creating cliques in the higher ranks of the Services. Allegations were made both in Parliament and outside that Menon was not following the usual procedure in regard to appointments and promotions, that many senior officers with creditable records had been superseded by juniors, and that the morale of the military had been adversely affected. The reports of the Auditor-General issued periodically also gave instances of waste in the Defence Ministry involving huge sums of money. Meanwhile, reports used to appear from time to time about China's aggressive intentions towards India, but Menon discounted them saying that Pakistan was the only power against which India had to guard herself.

Menon's work as Defence Minister was severely attacked in Parliament. Acharya Kripalani in a marathon speech on April 11, 1961 condemned him for his failure to strengthen the defence forces of the country, for creating schisms in the Services, and for squandering public money on wasteful schemes. He concluded his speech thus:

'I charge him with having created cliques in the Army. I charge him with having lowered the morale of our Armed forces; I charge him with having wasted the money of a poor and starving nation. I charge him with the neglect of the defence of the country against the aggression of Communist China. And in the international sphere, I charge him with having lent his support to the totalitarian and dictatorial regimes against the will of the people to freedom. May I, sir, at this critical moment appeal to Congressmen, who were not afraid of the British bullets and bayonets, to place the good of the nation above the supposed good of the party? I would remind how the Conservatives of England acted during the last war. They obliged even their Prime Minister Chamberlain to resign.'

Nehru, of course, strongly defended Menon. In fact, the more vehemently the latter was criticized, the more passionately he was supported by the Prime Minister. The Communist Party also stood by Menon. The opposition parties, excluding the communists, tried their best to defeat him in the election to the Lok Sabha from the North Bombay constituency in February 1962; but he won by a majority of more than one lakh votes over his rival Kripalani. Menon was then at the height of his power.

But in October 1962, when the Chinese launched their treacherous attack on India, our army was found wanting. It suffered a series of reverses and was easily routed by the Chinese. The whole country became indignant at the fact that a neigh-bour, believed to be a friendly power, had chosen to invade India, and that the Indian army was unable to give a good account of itself. It was alleged that although the Indian jawans were fighters of great ability, they were not properly equipped with weapons. Nor were they supplied even with adequate winter clothing and shoes. Menon naturally became the target of criti-cism, and public opinion demanded his dismissal. The agitation for his removal became so persistent that Nehru had to yield by taking over the Defence Portfolio himself and by making Menon responsible only for defence production. But the country was not to be satisfied with anything less than Menon's dismissal. Nehru explained that the responsibility for the army's reverses was not that of Menon alone but that of the entire Cabinet and, therefore, there was no point in asking for the removal of the Defence Minister. But such explanations, although constitution-ally correct, did not convince the critics. They were prepared to forgive Nehru but insisted on Menon's quitting the Cabinet; and curiously, it was the Congress Parliamentary Party that most vigorously pleaded for his removal. To what extent Menon had lost the confidence of his own Party will be evident from the following account of the meeting of the Executive Council of the Congress Parliamentary Party, given by the well-known American magazine *Time*:

'On November 7th, Nehru attended an all-day meeting of the Executive Committee of the Parliamentary Congress Party and made a fervent plea for Menon whose intellect, he said, was needed in the crisis. As a participant recalls it, ten clenched fists banged down on the table, a chorus of voices shouted, "No." Nehru was dumbfounded. It was he who was used to banging tables and making peremptory refusals. Taking a different track, he accurately said that he was as much at fault as Menon and vaguely threatened to resign. Always before, such a threat had been sufficient to make the opposition crumble with piteous cries of "Panditji, don't leave us alone!" This time, one of the leaders said: "If you continue to follow Menon's policies, we are prepared to contemplate that possibility." Nehru was beaten and Menon thrown out of the Cabinet.'

In his letter of resignation dated November 7, 1962, Menon observed

' . . . I am painfully aware of the fact that not only the opponents of our policy and party but even perhaps an appreciable number of our party members, some leaders among them, have proclaimed or implied their lack of faith in me and in the defence organization under my stewardship. These views may not, and in fact do not, represent the bulk of our party or the people. Nevertheless, in my humble submission, the reservations amid the crisis that are there, are a weak link in our national and party unity.'

Menon, therefore, submitted his resignation from the Cabinet 'in the belief that it may be a small contribution to the war effort.' Nehru while recommending the resignation to the President expressed his 'warm appreciation of the fine work' Menon had done in the Defence Ministry. Menon's resignation was followed by that of General P. N. Thapar, Chief of the Army Staff, on grounds of health.

UNUSUAL DEAL BETWEEN MINISTER AND MINE-OWNER

The resignation of K. D. Malaviya in 1963 was the first instance when a Cabinet Minister had to quit on charges of corruption. Malaviya joined the Council of Ministers as Deputy Minister of Natural Resources and Scientific Research in 1954. In 1957 he was promoted as Minister of State for Mines and Oil in which capacity he served for five years. In April 1962 he became a Cabinet Minister in charge of the same subjects. He displayed some vigour and initiative in developing the indigenous oil industry. India's requirements of petroleum were increasing rapidly on account of her intensive industrialization but until a few years ago, no serious and systematic efforts had been made to develop the country's oil resources and it had to depend heavily on imports. Today, India has made enormous progress on the road to self-sufficiency in petroleum products. Malaviya's policy was criticised because of its excessive bias in favour of the public sector. Progress in developing the oil industry, it was thought, could have been faster and more substantial if the oil companies in the private sector had not been fettered on ideological grounds.

Early in 1963 allegations were made both in Parliament and outside that Malaviya had accepted money from Serajuddin, a leading mine-owner and exporter of Calcutta, in return for certain concession from his ministry. Malaviya admitted having received Rs. 10,000/- from Serajuddin but he maintained that he took it for political, not personal, purposes, that is, for meeting the expenses of a Congress candidate who sought election to the U.P. Legislative Assembly. Malaviya emphatically denied that he had shown any favour to Serajuddin and he asserted that any concession that had been given was strictly in accordance with the rules framed under the Government's mineral policy. But this explanation did not convince Parliament and so Nehru referred the case for enquiry to Justice S. K. Das of the Supreme Court.

Unfortunately neither Parliament nor the public were taken into confidence in the matter of the enquiry. The findings of Justice Das were not made public because he had insisted, before he agreed to take up the enquiry, that they should not be published. All that the country was told was that out of the six allegations that were referred to Justice Das, two had gone against Malaviya and the rest in his favour. But no information was given as to what exactly was the nature of the allegations referred to Justice Das and which of them had gone against Malaviya. Nehru said in the Lok Sabha in August 1963 that

Justice Das had come to '*prima facie* conclusions' on the basis of the evidence before him and not to firm conclusions as a result of a regular trial. These '*prima facie* conclusions' influenced the Prime Minister in accepting Malaviya's resignation. In doing so, Nehru said that he was following those high principles of parliamentary government by which the office of a Minister was governed. He added, however, that he was not personally convinced that Malaviya had done anything which cast a reflection on his impartiality and integrity.

The Prime Minister's statement and his refusal to disclose the findings of Justice Das created confusion. Many wondered why Nehru accepted the resignation if he was thoroughly convinced of Malaviya's innocence.

Malaviya in his statement in the Lok Sabha on August 17, 1963 said that the method of enquiry had greatly handicapped him. It was of an informal and secret nature. The judge did not permit him to have the benefit of legal counsel during the examination of the witnesses. Some witnesses with direct knowledge of the facts were not even called. Further, the report of the judge was not to be published or discussed even in parliament but only used as personal advice to the Prime Minister.

'In these circumstances,' added Malaviya, 'the House will, I hope, appreciate the situation in which I am placed and permit me to say for the present that my conscience is clear. I can only assert my innocence and impartiality. There can be no question of my favouring anyone in any instance whatever.'

Malaviya's statement created the impression that he should have been given a fuller opportunity to defend himself. At the same time, many expressed surprise at the fact that Malaviya himself did not ask for such an opportunity.

RESIGNATIONS UNDER THE KAMARAJ PLAN HAD NOTHING TO DO WITH POLICY

We shall now deal with an entirely different type of resignations that took place in August 1963 under what is known as the Kamraj Plan. As we have already pointed out in chapter V the idea behind the Plan was that some senior leaders of the Congress should quit office and devote themselves to party work. Nehru accordingly accepted the resignation of Morarji Desai, the Finance Minister, S. K. Patil, the Minister for Food and Agriculture, Lal Bahadur Shastri, the Minister for Home Affairs, Jagjivan Ram, the Minister for Communications, Shrimali, Minister for Education, and Gopala Reddy, the Minister for Information and Broadcasting. Although these ministers were apparently relieved for doing party work, it was widely believed that Nehru availed himself of the opportunity of the Kamaraj Plan to get rid of inconvenient or incompetent colleagues whom he could not remove in the normal way. Thus S. K. Patil was dropped, it was believed, because he had failed to improve the food situation and he was also unwilling to change over to another portfolio as desired by the Prime Minister. Morarji Desai had become unpopular because of gold control and the compulsory desposit scheme. Moreover, both Patil and Desai had incurred the wrath of the communists who had strongly and specifically urged for their dismissal from the Cabinet during the debate on the no-confidence motion in August 1963. The communists' argument was that with the exit earlier of Krishna Menon and Malaviya, the ideological balance in the Cabinet had been gravely disturbed and that so long as Patil and Desai remained in power, the Cabinet would be heavily dominated by the Right. Such views were also expressed by *Pravda*, the Soviet newspaper, and Nehru, always sensitive to criticism from Moscow, readily agreed to drop his two most controversial colleagues.

The acceptance of the resignation of the other ministers was also believed to be due to specific reasons. Gopala Reddy's resignation was connected with the 'Voice of America' deal which had caused considerable embarrassment to Nehru. Shrimali was supposed to have been relieved because he had done nothing remarkable as Minister for Education. Jagjivan Ram's going caused little surprise since he had been a Cabinet Minister continuously for sixteen years. As regards Lal Bahadur Shastri it was thought that Nehru agreed to drop him because the Prime Minister was anxious to keep up an appearance of impartiality in accepting these resignations and, moreover, he wanted him to take over the Congress Presidency which was assuming considerable importance.

Nehru, of course, denied that the resignations were due to

policy difference or because of his desire to get rid of certain colleagues for personal or ideological reasons.[1] His explanation was that the Kamaraj Plan would make an impact on the public only if a number of senior ministers gave up office and devoted themselves to party work. He told the Lok Sabha on August 30, 1963:

'Rather unusual circumstance led to the resignation of some of our seniormost and most respected members of the House and of the Government . . . It is with regret that I recommend to the President that these resignations be accepted. In our Government it will make a big difference without senior and experienced members whose advice counted so much. I would only add that this has nothing to do with any questions of policy that usually lead to resignations. The reasons were entirely different. However, I am glad that although they have resigned from the Cabinet they will continue as members of this House and we shall continue to have the advantage of their advice and co-operation.'

[1] Consider, in this context, Attlee's principle in selecting his Cabinet colleagues. 'The fatal mistake', he told his biographer, 'is to select only people you think are docile yes-men. You must put in people who are likely to be awkward. I did.'

CHAPTER VII

RELATIONS
WITH RASHTRAPATHI[1]

The office of the Indian President is a unique institution. His status and functions are neither like those of the British Monarch nor of the American President although the Indian Constitution incorporates important features from the Constitutions of both these countries. In order to understand his position correctly, it is necessary to recall the background in which the Constitution of India was framed in 1946-9.

Having provided for a quasi-federal structure, the fathers of the Constitution were anxious to ensure that the Head of the State was not an ornamental figure nor, at the same time, was he made as powerful as the American President. As K. M. Munshi, who played a prominent part in framing the Constitution, says,

'The provisions were the outcome of a definite decision that the President should not be the creature of the Parliament nor the nominee of the party in power at the centre, nor a figurehead as the President of the French Constitution of 1875, but an independent organ of the State representing the whole Union and exercising independent powers.'

MODE OF ELECTION

The Indian President is chosen by indirect election. The Constituent Assembly decided against direct election because it was considered unnecessary since under the parliamentary system of government, the real power would vest in the Cabinet and not in the President. Moreover, direct election would be a costly and cumbrous procedure, involving the exercise of franchise by a vast

[1] Rashtrapathi, a Hindi word, means President of the Indian Republic.

electorate of over 300 million people. So the President is elected by an electoral college consisting of the elected members of both Houses of Parliament and the elected members of the legislative assemblies of the States. The election is held in accordance with the system of proportional representation by means of the single transferable vote, the voting being done by secret ballot. A candidate for election as President should be an Indian citizen, should have completed thirty-five years of age, be qualified for election as a member of the Lok Sabha,[1] and shall not hold any office for profit. On entering upon his office, he has to take a solemn oath affirming that: 'I will faithfully execute the office of the President . . . to the best of my ability, preserve, protect and defend the Constitution and the law and that I will devote myself to the service and well-being of the people of India.' The President is elected for a term of five years but he is eligible for re-election. There are two ways by which he may quit office within the term of five years; by tendering his resignation in writing addressed to the Vice-President of India or by removal by impeachment for violating the Constitution.

POWERS OF THE PRESIDENT

The President's powers fall broadly into three categories: executive, legislative, and judicial.

Under Article 53 of the Constitution, the executive powers of the Union are vested in the President and shall be exercised by him either directly or through officers subordinate to him in accordance with the Constitution. He has a Council of Ministers to 'aid and advise' him in the exercise of his functions. He appoints the Prime Minister and, on the latter's advice, the other ministers. The ministers shall hold office during the pleasure of the President,[2] and he administers the oath of office and of secrecy.

[1] But the President shall not be a member of either House of Parliament or of any State legislature.
[2] In practice, as we have seen earlier, the choice of ministers is solely at the discretion of the Prime Minister. The President is bound to appoint as Prime Minister the leader of the majority Party in the Lok Sabha and accept his nominees as ministers.

Article 77 lays down that

'all executive action of the Government of India shall be expressed to be taken in the name of the President, that all orders and other instruments made and executed in the name of the President shall be authenticated in such manner as may be specified in rules to be made by the President and the validity of an order or instrument which is so authenticated shall not be called in question on the ground that it is not an order or instrument made or executed by the President.'

The Constitution empowers the President to make rules for the more convenient transaction of the Government of India and for the allocation of business among ministers. It also enjoins upon the Prime Minister to

'communicate to the President all decisions of the Council of Ministers relating to the administration of the affairs of the Union and proposals for legislation; to furnish such information relating to the administration of the affairs of the Union and proposals for legislation as the President may call for: and if the President so requires, to submit for the consideration of the Council of Ministers any matter on which a decision has been taken by a Minister but which has not been considered by the Council.'

The President also appoints, on the advice of the Cabinet, the Attorney-General of the Union, the Comptroller and Auditor-General, the judges of the Supreme Court[1] and High Courts, the Chairman and members of the Union Public Service Commission and the State Governors. He also appoints the Union Public Service Commission, the Chief Election Commissioner, the Finance Commission, a Commission to enquire into the administration of scheduled areas, a Commission to study the condition of the backward classes, and so on.

The legislative powers of the President are the following: he may summon the Houses or either House to meet at such time and place as he thinks fit; he may prorogue the House and

---

[1] While appointing judges of the Supreme Court, the President has to consult also the Chief Justice of the Supreme Court.

dissolve the House of the people. He may address either House of Parliament or both Houses together. He may send messages to either House of Parliament whether with respect to a bill pending in Parliament or otherwise. His assent is necessary for bills passed by Parliament to become law. He may also return a bill, which is not a money bill, to the House with his suggestions for reconsideration; and if the bill is again passed with or without the suggested amendments, the President has no power to withhold his assent. The President also has the power to disallow bills passed by a State Legislature and reserved for his assent; or he may send them back to the Governor for reconsideration by the legislature.

The President shall cause to be laid, in respect of every financial year, the annual financial statement, showing separately the sums required to meet expenditure described by the Constitution as expenditure charged upon the Consolidated Fund of India, and the sums required to meet other expenditure proposed to be made from the Consolidated Fund. The President also shall cause certain reports to be placed before Parliament, such as the report of the Auditor-General concerning the accounts of the Government of India, the report of the Finance Commission together with a memorandum explaining the action taken thereon, the report of the Union Public Service Commission, the report of the Special Officer for Scheduled Castes and Tribes, the report of the Commission on backward classes; and the report of the Special Officer for linguistic minorities.

The President has the power to issue ordinances when he is satisfied that circumstances exist which render it necessary for him to take immediate action. Every such ordinance must be laid before both Houses of Parliament and it will cease to operate at the expiry of six weeks after the re-assembly of Parliament, or earlier if disapproved by both Houses. The President also may withdraw the ordinance.

The ordinance making power of the President has been criticized by some persons on the ground that it encroaches on the sovereignty of Parliament. But this criticism is not justified because the President can exercise this power only on the advice of the Cabinet, and not in his discretion, and only when Parliament is not in session.

The judicial powers of the President include the right to grant pardons, reprieves, respites or remissions of punishment or to suspend, remit or commute the sentence on persons convicted by court martial and in cases in which the sentence of death has been passed. The President also has the power to refer any question of public importance to the Supreme Court for its opinion.

Apart from the normal powers of the President described above, he has been endowed with certain emergency powers, broadly of three categories. The President may issue a proclamation of emergency when he is satisfied that the security of India, or any part thereof, has been threatened by war, external aggression or internal disorder. Such a proclamation must be laid before each House of Parliament. It will cease to operate at the expiry of two months unless before that period it has been approved by both Houses of Parliament. The effect of the proclamation is that, for all practical purposes during the period of the emergency, the State Governments will be under the complete control of the Central Government. The latter is empowered to give directions to any State Government regarding the manner in which its executive power is to be exercised; and Parliament will have the power to legislate on subjects in the State List as well. The financial relations between the Centre and the States may also be suitably modified if necessary by Presidential order. Moreover, so long as the emergency is in force, the right of citizens to move the Courts for the enforcement of fundamental rights remains suspended. For the first time the President issued a proclamation of emergency under Article 352 on October 26, 1962 when India was invaded by China; and the proclamation continues to be in force till the time of writing.

The second type of emergency relates to the failure of constitutional machinery in the States: when the President is satisfied that the administration of a State cannot be carried on in accordance with the Constitution, he may issue a proclamation under Article 356 by which the Central Government may take over all the functions, except judicial, of the State. Such proclamations have been issued on four occasions in Kerala in 1956, in 1959, in 1964, and in 1965; and also once in the Punjab in 1950 and in Andhra in 1954.

The President is also empowered under Article 360 to issue a proclamation when he is satisfied that the financial stability or credit of India or of any part of the territory thereof is threatened. When such a proclamation is in operation, the Central Government has the power to issue directions to any State to observe suitable canons of financial propriety, which may include a provision requiring the reduction of salaries and allowances of all or any class of persons serving in connection with the affairs of the Union, including judges of the Supreme Court and High Courts as well as of a State Government. The proclamation may also require all money bills or other financial Bills to be reserved for the consideration of the President after they are passed by the State Legislature.

The Constitution also vests the supreme command of the Defence Forces of the Indian Union in the President, but he will exercise the powers in this respect in accordance with the law.

PRESIDENT'S SECRETARIAT

The President is assisted by two secretaries. One is designated as Secretary to the President and the other as Military Secretary to the President. Each Secretary has his separate establishment. The Secretary to the President is usually a very senior member of the Civil Service. He provides the liaison between the President and the Departments of the Government of India. He places before the President all papers that require his sanction or instructions, and conveys them to the appropriate departments. The Secretary also arranges interviews with the President and looks after the President's correspondence with State Governors as well as with the various non-official or semi-official organizations with which he is connected.

The main work of the Military Secretary is to make suitable arrangements for all functions that take place in the Rashtrapathi Bhawan or the Prime Minister's House, to draw up the tour programme of the President, to allot accommodation in the President's Estate and in the Rashtrapathi Bhawan, and to supervise the arrangements in connection with entertainments given by the President, Vice-President or the Prime Minister.

HOW THE PRESIDENT USES HIS POWERS

It is thus clear that the Indian Constitution vests the President[1] with vast powers over vital aspects of the administration. However, opinion seems divided among constitutional experts about the actual status of the President. Some argue that whatever the Constitution may say, in practice, the President can, and should, act only in accordance with the advice of the Cabinet in the interests of smooth administration. But others hold the view that if the President were to act always in accordance with the wishes of the Cabinet, it will ultimately result in the destruction of democracy. It will be useful to summarize briefly both these points of view.

The exponents of the first school of thought suggest that although the Constitution does not specifically lay down that the President should act always on the advice of the Cabinet, it was expected by the authors of the Constitution that he would conduct himself on the model of the British monarch so as to maintain the sovereignty of the Indian Parliament. If the President did not do so, it would mean that Parliament would not be supreme, for under the Constitution, the actions of the President could not be discussed in Parliament.

It is interesting to recall that the Constituent Assembly had originally intended to incorporate in the Constitution an instrument of instructions, making it obligatory on the President to act always in accordance with the advice of the Cabinet. The instruction proposed was as follows: 'In all matters within the scope of the executive power of the Union, the President shall, in the exercise of the powers conferred upon him, be guided by the advice of his ministers.' But subsequently this proposal was dropped. B. N. Rau points out in his *Indian Constitution in the Making* that a number of members of the Constituent Assembly

[1] The Constitution provides for a Vice-President who is *ex-officio* the Chairman of the Rajya Sabha. He is elected by members of both Houses of Parliament assembled at a joint meeting in accordance with the system of proportional representation. The Vice-President shall act as President in the event of any vacancy caused by the latter's death, resignation, or removal until the new President is elected. But the Vice-President does not automatically become the President when a permanent vacancy occurs. He merely acts as President till the election is held. The Vice-President, when he acts as President, shall have all the powers of the President.

objected to this proposal being dropped because it was not clear how far the conventions of the British Constitution would be binding under the Indian Constitution. But the Law Minister categorically assured them that the conventions would be binding on parliament. He was specifically asked: 'If in any particular case the President does not act upon the advice of his Council of Ministers, will that be tantamount to a violation of the Constitution and will he be liable to impeachment?' To this question the Law Minister's answer was: 'There is not the slightest doubt about it.' The Constituent Assembly, on this assurance, agreed to omit the clause.

B. N. Rau also makes the important point that 'acting on ministerial advice does not necessarily mean the immediate acceptance of the Ministry's first thoughts. The President can state all his objections to any proposed course of action and ask his ministers in Council, if necessary, to reconsider the matter. It is only in the last resort that he should accept their final advice.'

Rajendra Prasad also expressed the view in the Constituent Assembly that the President should conduct himself as a constitutional monarch. He said:

'Although there is no specific provision in the Constitution itself making it binding on the President to accept the advice of his ministers, it is hoped that the convention, under which in England the king always acted on the advice of his ministers, would be established in this country also and that the President would become a constitutional President in all matters.'

But other eminent constitutional experts, including Patanjali Sastri, a former Chief Justice of the Supreme Court, have asserted that the President is under no obligation to act always on the advice of his ministers. The Constitution, they argue, has provided for a Council of Ministers to aid and advise the President but nowhere is it laid down, as it has been done in the Irish Constitution, that he should always be guided by them. They point out that unlike as in Britain, the Indian Constitution provides for a quasi-federation where there is a clear demarcation of powers between the Centre and the States. Both the Central and

State Legislatures participate in the election of the President, who has the responsibility to ensure the autonomy of the States against encroachment from the Centre. 'If the powers of the President are passed on to the Prime Minister and the President becomes a figure-head,' says K. M. Munshi, 'the character of the Union as a quasi-federation will be destroyed. The Union will become a unitary one and its powers of maintaining the unity of the country will also be materially impaired.'

The exponents of this view quote in their support Article 61 which provides for impeachment of the President if he violates the Constitution. The charge can be initiated by either House of Parliament, after giving at least fourteen days' notice in writing, signed by no fewer than one fourth of the total number of members of the House, and the resolution should be passed by a majority of not less than two-thirds of the total membership of the House. A charge so preferred by either House of Parliament will be investigated by the other House and the President has the right to appear and to be represented at such investigation. The President will be removed from office if, as a result of the investigation, a resolution is passed by a majority of not less than two-thirds of the total membership of the House by which the charge was investigated, sustaining the charge against him.

In view of this clear provision for impeachment, it is suggested that the President has a personal responsibility to preserve and protect the Constitution—a responsibility which cannot be passed on to the Cabinet. It is, therefore, contended that there is not, and cannot be any legal obligation on the President to accept the advice of the ministers. Munshi in fact argues that some of the President's powers are 'super-ministerial' where the Cabinet 'could not be relied upon to advise him'. These include the power to dismiss a Prime Minister who does not enjoy the leadership of the Party, to remove a ministry which has lost the confidence of the Parliament, to dissolve the Lok Sabha when it ceases to command the confidence of the people, and to exercise the authority of the Supreme Commander in an emergency where the ministry has failed to defend the country. Munshi also recalls the opinion expressed by Nehru in the Constituent Assembly: 'We did not want the President to be just a mere figurehead like the French President.'

PRESIDENT AND PRIME MINISTER

From the strictly constitutional point of view, Munshi's interpretation seems correct.[1] But what ultimately matters is the
personality of the President as well as his personal relationship
with the Prime Minister. So far, the Constitution has worked
smoothly because of the cordial relationship between the President and the Prime Minister and because the same political party,
namely the Congress, has been in power both at the Centre and
in the States ever since the Constitution came into force in
January 1950.[2]

India's first President was Rajendra Prasad, a veteran Congressman and a close associate of Mahatma Gandhi. Before the attainment of freedom, Prasad had served as the Congress President for
three terms and as a member of the Congress Working Committee for a number of years. He was Minister of Food and Agriculture in the Interim Government of India set up in September
1946 but resigned the post on being elected President of the
Constituent Assembly. His election as President of the Indian
Republic in January 1950 was opposed by the late Professor K. T.
Shah, an eminent economist. But Prasad was elected by 2,896
votes out of the total of 3,486 votes cast.

Prasad and Nehru had been intimate colleagues in the Congress for many decades and both had great respect and affection
for each other, although their outlook on political and economic
problems was not always identical. While Nehru favoured radical

[1] The following comments on the President's constitutional position, made
by India's Supreme Court, in Ram Jawaya v. State of Punjab (1955), are significant: 'Under Article 53(1) of our Constitution, the executive power of the
Union is vested in the President, but under Article 75 there is to be a Council
of Ministers with the Prime Minister at the head to aid and advise on his
functions. The President has thus been made a formal head of the executive
and the real executive powers are vested in the Ministers or the Cabinet. The
same provisions obtain in regard to the Government of States: the Governor
occupies the position of the head of the executive in the State, but it is vir-
tually the Council of Ministers in each State that carries on the executive
Government. In the Indian Constitution therefore we have the same system
of parliamentary executive as in England, and the Council of Ministers, consisting as it does of the members of the Legislature, is like the British Cabinet
—"a hyphen which joins, a buckle which fastens the legislative part of the
State to the executive part".'
[2] In Kerala, however, the communist party was in power for a brief period
of twenty-seven months in 1957-9.

and rapid reforms in the country's economic and social structure, Prasad wanted to go slow so that the Government could carry public opinion with it. It was, therefore, unsurprising that sometimes differences arose between the President and the Prime Minister on certain major issues.

For instance, when the Government wanted in 1950 to rush through the Hindu Code Bill, which sought to bring about drastic changes in the marriage and property laws of Hindus, Prasad advised the Prime Minister against its hasty legislation. The President's view was that there was no urgency to take up the reform of only one community and that, moreover, the Constituent Assembly did not have the mandate from the people to introduce social legislation of a revolutionary nature. The Bill met with strong opposition both from within the Congress and other sections of public opinion and the Government, therefore, was compelled to postpone its consideration.

Food policy was another major question on which the President and the Prime Minister did not see eye to eye. The Government's proposals to impose ceilings on landholdings, to introduce co-operative farming and to resort to State trading in foodgrains created uncertainty in the country, particularly in the rural areas. Prasad, who had an intimate acquaintance with India's agricultural problems, felt that these measures were likely to disrupt production, dislocate the trade and dampen initiative and enthusiasm on the part of the people, especially among those engaged in agricultural pursuits. Therefore, in a letter to the Prime Minister in June 1959, Prasad gave expression to these views and advised a reconsideration of the proposals. He pointed out that food production should not be mixed with the programme of social legislation. State trading in foodgrains would result in multiplying and aggravating difficulties because, apart from other factors, it required a tremendous organization and trained personnel. He urged the encouragement of the existing large agricultural farms for utilizing mechanized methods. He also recommended the formation of service co-operatives of small farmers by providing the necessary credit, improved seeds and irrigation facilities. The President added that positive action to discourage hoarding would achieve better results than the price control.

Nehru in his reply welcomed the President's suggestions and pointed out that while State trading in foodgrains had resulted in immediate difficulties, including an increase in prices, the Government had no alternative. He also laid emphasis on the service co-operatives though he would like co-operative farming to develop gradually.

Although the correspondence between the President and the Prime Minister was meant to be strictly confidential, its contents leaked to the Press; and K. L. Punjabi, who was Secretary to the President, records in his biography of Prasad, that the publication of the President's letter

'strengthened the hands of the State governments which were reluctant to undertake State trading . . . The President's views were generally supported by the Press and by thoughtful people, among whom were numbered many Congressmen whose voices could not be heard in the party.'

Another important letter from the President to the Prime Minister, which also found its way into the newspapers, was in regard to corruption in high places. C. D. Deshmukh, a former Finance Minister, had suggested, in a speech in Madras towards the end of 1959, the need for a high-powered tribunal to examine the charges of corruption against ministers and other influential persons. He also asserted that he had concrete evidence to confirm charges of corruption, against some top people in the government but he would disclose it only to an independent tribunal. Prasad observed that the Government should consider seriously Deshmukh's suggestion and take prompt and effective measures to root out corruption. Nehru, however, regretted his inability to set up a tribunal although he fully shared the President's anxiety to put down corruption.

The introduction of Hindi for official purposes was another major issue on which the Prime Minister and the President differed. Prasad felt that the use of Hindi in Government offices should be speedily and vigorously encouraged so that it might become the sole official language as early as possible. Nehru, on the other hand, was of opinion that the Government should not force the pace of Hindi in offices because, first, there were practical difficulties in using it at all levels of administration and, secondly, such a course would meet with stiff opposition from non-Hindi areas, especially from the South.

These instances clearly show that India's first President did not function like a figure-head and that he did try to influence the Cabinet on major decisions. In fact, Prasad even suggested in his address to the Indian Law Association in 1961 that there was need to consider what exactly were the powers enjoyed by the President under the Constitution. The President's remarks caused some surprise in the country because he himself had played a conspicuous part in framing the Indian Constitution, and many wondered what was the purpose in having the relevant provisions examined. When Nehru enquired of Prasad as to what it was all about, the latter was reported to have told the Prime Minister that it was only a casual suggestion he had made while addressing a gathering of lawyers.

Although the President and the Prime Minister did differ on some major issues, the relationship between them was perfectly cordial; and when Prasad retired in May 1962 the Prime Minister and Parliament paid him warm tributes for the ability and tact with which he had conducted himself in this high office for twelve years. The address presented to him on May 8, 1962, said

'By your qualities of unostentatious grace, your utter simplicity, clarity of outlook, deep humility and broad humanity, you invested a special meaning and significance in your choice as President. As the first President of India, you have enriched and embellished the office and are leaving behind inspiring traditions.'

Prasad was succeeded by S. Radhakrishnan who had served as Vice-President of India since 1952. As scholar, professor and philosopher, he had won great renown both in India and abroad. He had also been India's Ambassador in Moscow for three years. Within a few months after his election as President of India came the massive invasion by China in October 1962, and the President, therefore, proclaimed an Emergency in November under Article 352 of the Constitution.

During the four years he has been President, Radhakrishnan has shown courage and statesmanship of a high order. He made no secret of the fact that the Chinese invasion had greatly hurt the prestige of India. In a speech in Bombay in January 1963, he described India's reverses in NEFA as 'a matter of sorrow, shame and humiliation'. His speeches in the United States and the United Kingdom, which he visited in 1963, helped to create a better understanding of India's foreign policy, and strengthened India's friendship with the Western world.

Radhakrishnan often has been quite frank in expressing his views on important problems. For example, in his address to the first convocation of the Uttar Pradesh Agricultural University in November 1963, he attributed the stagnation in India's agriculture to administrative inefficiency. India's farmers, he said, were intelligent, capable of accepting new methods, and applying them to the development of agriculture. So, if the farmers were good and the land was there and the Government was improving the irrigation facilities, what was it that had led to this deterioration in agricultural production? The President raised this question and pointed out that the failure in agriculture indicated nothing more than 'lack of true, wise leadership and administrative efficiency.'

Again in his broadcast to the nation on Republic Day in January 1964, Radhakrishnan cautioned the country against complacency towards corruption. 'It would be well to recognize,' he said, 'that the tolerance of our society for weak, inefficient and unclean administration is not unlimited.'

As in the case of India's first President, Nehru and Radhakrishnan also got on together very well indeed. In his Republic Day message in January 1964, Radhakrishnan expressed his pleasure and that of the people of India in Nehru's rapid recovery from his illness, and paid a warm tribute to the Prime Minister's leadership. The President said: 'He has brought a modern, secular and scientific outlook to our difficult and diverse problems and has, indeed, reflected the national purpose over these years. More than anyone, our Prime Minister has helped us to put us on the right track in our quest for national integration and orderly growth.' And on the death of Nehru, the President, in the course of a broadcast to the nation, said:

'Nehru held the office of the Prime Minister of our country ever since the dawn of independence; and in the long years of his Premiership, tried to put our country on a progressive, scientific, dynamic and non-communal basis. His steadfast loyalty to certain fundamental principles of liberalism gave direction to our thought and life . . . He used the existing social and political institutions and breathed into them a new spirit, a new vitality.'[1]

The war with Pakistan was the major event during the eighteen-month tenure of Shastri as the Prime Minister. During the twenty-two days when the fighting went on, the President kept himself in close touch with the military developments and gave his full support to the Prime Minister. As the Supreme Commander, the President encouraged the armed forces to give of their best and also inspired the people through broadcasts to keep their morale high. And when the cease-fire was proclaimed on September 22nd, he publicly congratulated Shastri and the Chiefs of Staff. He said:

'I should like to congratulate our Prime Minister and the Government and our Chiefs of Staff, General Chaudhuri, Air Marshal Arjan Singh and Vice-Admiral Soman, on the hard and excellent work which they and those working under their leadership have done in these difficult days. We have today retrieved our prestige and it is my hope that our Army, Air Force and Navy will continue to function with daring, heroism and skill and be treated as a force to be reckoned with.'

[1] The role of the President in forming a caretaker government, following the death of Nehru, has been described in Chapter X.

CHAPTER VIII

PLANNING COMMISSION—
SUPER CABINET?

Ever since the Planning Commission was set up in May 1950, its composition, status, powers and functions have been subjected to much criticism. In fact, at the time when the Commission was constituted, there was no unanimity within the Cabinet itself about the need and scope for an independent planning body. Sardar Patel, the Deputy Prime Minister, did not like it and Dr John Mathai, the Finance Minister, vigorously opposed its formation. The latter argued that the Commission was unnecessary at that stage and that it was likely to encroach on the authority of the Cabinet. Dr. Mathai felt so strongly about it that he resigned from the Cabinet on this issue, as we saw in a preceding chapter.

Public opinion in India is practically unanimous about the need for some agency for planning the country's economy on the right lines. No responsible leader or political party has called in question the necessity for a plan or a planning body. But serious differences prevail about the manner in which planning is to be undertaken. On the one hand, there are the socialists and communists who want the economy to be brought increasingly under rigid State control and who, therefore, favour planning on a comprehensive scale. On the other hand, there are parties like the Swatantra which admit the need for planning but want it to be done in such a way as to promote individual initiative and enterprise.

The Congress, since the thirties, has been staunchly advocating a planned economy for India. In 1938 when Subhas Bose was the Congress President, a National Planning Committee was formed, under the Chairmanship of Nehru, for drawing up a plan for the country's economic development. It was a fifteen-member Committee which included eminent economists, industrialists and scientists as well as nominees of the provincial governments. As Nehru says, it was 'a remarkably representative committee cutting across political boundaries as well as the high barrier between official and non-official India, except for the fact that the Government of India was not represented.' The Committee set up nearly thirty sub-committees to make detailed studies of different problems. The Committee's work was interrupted by the outbreak of the second world war. But it did valuable service by producing a series of reports that helped to focus attention on the weak spots of the economy.

The war considerably disrupted our economy but at the same time it stimulated discussion among the leaders regarding the ways and means to be adopted for achieving rapid economic progress. For example, the Bombay Plan sponsored in 1944 by prominent industrialists, recommended an investment of Rs. 10,000 crores in a fifteen-year period for doubling the per capita income. The Government of India also began to give serious attention to the problem of economic development. It constituted in 1944 a Planning and Development Department and an Advisory Planning Board in 1946. The details of the Bombay Plan, or of the work done by the official committees, do not concern us here. What is important to note is that by the time of transfer of power in 1947, the country as a whole had become conscious of the imperative need for an intelligent and integrated plan to bring about the rapid improvement of the economy. It was inevitable, therefore, that soon after the achievement of freedom, the Government of India should think of setting up a separate and independent organization for preparing detailed schemes for economic development.

PLANNING OBJECTIVES

The Planning Commission was accordingly established in 1950. 'The need for comprehensive planning based on a careful appraisal of resources and an objective analysis of all the relevant factors has become imperative,' said the Government of India, in its resolution of March 15, 1950, announcing the formation of the Planning Commission. 'These purposes,' it added, 'can best be achieved through an organization free from the burden of day-to-day administration, but in constant touch with the

Government at the highest level.' The Commission was enjoined to: (a) make an assessment of the material, capital and human resources of the country, including technical personnel, and investigate the possibilities of augmenting such of these resources as are found to be deficient in relation to the nation's requirements;

(b) to formulate a Plan for the most effective and balanced utilization of the country's resources;

(c) on a determination of priorities, define the stages in which the Plan should be carried out and propose the allocation of resources for the due completion of each stage;

(d) indicate the factors which are tending to retard economic development, and determine the conditions which, in view of the current social and political situation, should be established for the successful execution of the Plan;

(e) determine the nature of the machinery which will be necessary for securing the successful implementation of each stage of the Plan in all its aspects;

(f) appraise from time to time the progress achieved in the execution of each stage of the Plan and recommend the adjustments of policy and measures that such appraisal may show to be necessary; and

(g) make such interim or ancillary recommendations as appear to it to be appropriate either for facilitating the discharge of the duties assigned to it; or on a consideration of the prevailing economic conditions, current policies, measures and development programme; or on an examination of such specific problems as may be referred to it for advice by Central or State Governments.

MEMBERSHIP OF COMMISSION

The Commission started functioning in March 1950 with Nehru as Chairman and five full-time members. These were G. L. Nanda, V. T. Krishnamachari, G. L. Mehta, R. K. Patil and C. D. Deshmukh. All of them had vast experience in different fields of activity. Nanda had for many years specialized in problems of industrial labour. Krishnamachari had distinguished himself as a competent administrator in British India and in Indian States. Mehta had an intimate knowledge of business and finance. Both

Deshmukh and Patil had been in the Indian Civil Service and had first-hand knowledge of administrative problems. To start with, the Prime Minister was the only link with the Cabinet. In May 1950, Deshmukh joined the Cabinet as Finance Minister but he continued to retain his membership of the Planning Commission. Since then the Finance Minister has always been a member of the Planning Commission. In September 1951 Nanda also joined the Cabinet as Minister for Planning but continued to work as the Deputy Chairman of the Planning Commission till February 1953 when V. T. Krishnamachari was appointed to this post. The Commission was further strengthened in 1956 with the appointment of V. K. Krishna Menon, Defence Minister and Professor P. C. Mahalanobis, the Honorary Statistical Adviser to the Cabinet. The composition of the Commission underwent some changes in the subsequent years, and at the time of Nehru's death it consisted of eleven members besides the Prime Minister, namely: Asoka Mehta, Shriman Narayan, T. N. Singh, P. C. Mahalanobis, M. S. Thacker, Tarlok Singh, V. K. R. V. Rao, G. L. Nanda, T. T. Krishnamachari, Swaran Singh and B. R. Bhagat.

No specific qualifications and experience have been laid down for membership; the appointments are made by the Prime Minister in consultation with the Deputy Chairman of the Planning Commission. There is also no fixed tenure for members. Since 1953 full-time members have been given salaries and allowances on the same scale as Ministers of State. There are no definite rules in regard to the distribution of portfolios among members of the Commission. This often depends on the background and special interests of the members concerned.

HOW BIG IS THE COMMISSION

The Planning Commission started on a modest scale but in course of time it developed into a huge organization. At present it consists of two co-ordinating Divisions, six General Divisions and twelve Subject Divisions. The Co-ordinating Divisions are: the Programme Administration Division and the Plan Co-ordination Division. The General Divisions deal with financial resources, economic policy and foreign trade; perspective planning; labour and employment; statistics and surveys; natural resources and scientific research; and management and administration. The Subject Divisions are concerned with agriculture, co-operation and community development; irrigation and power; land reforms; industry and minerals; village and small industries; transport and communication; education; health; housing; social welfare; rural works; and public co-operation. Besides, there are a large number of committees and panels to advise the Commission.[1] The total expenditure on the Planning Commission has also gone up sharply from Rs. 8.56 lakhs in 1950-51 to Rs. 67.02 lakhs in 1964-5 (estimated). The increase in expenditure during this period on the pay of officers was from Rs. 3,19,354 to Rs. 30,05,500; pay of establishment from Rs. 1,57,676 to Rs. 18,66,800; allowances and honorariums from Rs. 2,01,685 to Rs. 13,27,700; and other charges from Rs. 1,77,821 to Rs. 5,00,000.

HOW THE COMMISSION WORKS

The Planning Commission works in close consultation with the Cabinet. The Prime Minister and other Ministers, who are members of the Commission, attend all meetings of the Commission at which major issues are discussed. Similarly, the Deputy Chairman and members of the Planning Commission attend meetings of the Cabinet and its Committees when discussions take place on important matters connected with Planning. Thus as V. T. Krishnamachari says, in his book, *Fundamentals of Planning in India,*

'there is close and continuous touch between the Planning Commission, on the one hand, and the Ministers and the Cabinet and Cabinet Committees on the other. This places the Commission under a two-fold obligation: first, it has to maintain secrecy in regard to differences of views between the Commission and Union and State Ministers. It cannot give out what its recommendations are and to what extent these are accepted or rejected;

[1] For a detailed account of the Commission's organization, see *The Planning Commission* by H. K. Paranjape (The Indian Institute of Public Administration).

secondly, it cannot engage in controversies in public about the Plan, or reply directly to criticisms. It is for the Government concerned to decide in individual cases what information they would like to place before the public.'

The Commission is supposed to be only an advisory body. Its recommendations are not necessarily accepted by the Cabinet, despite the fact that the Prime Minister and some of his colleagues holding key portfolios are also members of the Commission. Nevertheless, in practice, the Commission has over the years grown greatly in strength, power and influence. Until January 1964, the Cabinet Secretary also acted as Secretary to the Commission; and many senior officers of the Government have been closely associated with the work of the Commission at various stages. The State Governments too have come to rely increasingly on the Commission for economic advice and financial assistance.

The composition and working of the Planning Commission have come in for criticism from various quarters—from Parliament and State legislatures, official committees, industrial organizations, academic bodies, individual economists and, above all, from Nehru himself. It is necessary to examine some of the arguments of the critics in order to find out to what extent the Commission has helped or hindered the country's economic progress.

The most weighty and detailed criticism of the Commission has come from the Estimates Committee of the Lok Sabha. The Committee carefully enquired into all aspects of the Commission's working and, in its report submitted in April 1958, made a number of recommendations. The Committee recognized the difficulties inherent in planning in a federal state but suggested that the Commission should be so organized as to eliminate delays, avoid duplication, ensure co-ordination and produce results. It referred to the generally prevalent feeling that the Planning Commission was not just an advisory body but an additional authority to be reckoned with, which, though not part of the ordinary machinery of the Government of India, decided every programme of work and whose decisions were to be carried out by all. The Committee noted that the need to consult the Commission and obtain its sanctions sometimes caused delays and dissatisfaction. The Committee did not consider it essential that the Prime Minister should be formally associated with the Planning Commission although such a connection was 'absolutely necessary' in the formative stages, and his guidance would still be necessary for the success of planning.

As regards the association of other ministers with the Commission, the Committee felt that it was not necessary to continue this practice and that adequate co-ordination could be achieved by inviting the Cabinet Minister concerned to attend the meetings of the Planning Commission and by inviting the members of the Planning Commission to attend the Cabinet meetings when necessary.

The practice of having a common secretary both for the Commission and the Cabinet was also criticized by the Committee. The Cabinet Secretary, it was pointed out, had very little time to devote to the Planning Commission whose responsibilities were rapidly increasing; moreover this arrangement did not help to secure 'a freshness of outlook and independence of judgment.' It was essential, therefore, that the Commission should have a whole-time Secretary.

The other important recommendations of the Committee were that the 'anomalous' position of Professor Mahalanobis should be rectified, that the allocation of work among the various Divisions,[1] should be done on a rational basis, that the Organization and Methods section which, in the previous two years, had done no useful work, should function actively, that the Commission should be divested of executive powers like sanctioning grants-in-aid to public bodies, and that posts should be sanctioned only when they were fully justified. However, many of the main recommendations of the Committee have not been implemented.

Professor D. R. Gadgil, Director of the Gokhale Institute of Politics and Economics, Poona, in his Laski Memorial Lectures

[1] The Committee's comments on the composition of the Land Reforms Division are significant. It said: 'Among the staff working in this Division, there is no person who has personal experience of land tenures and their problems in the States. The Committee feel that the absence of experienced people in this Division might, to a certain extent, account for the lack of progress in regard to land reforms work. They recommend that persons who have field experience as well as academic attainments and have attained the necessary status should be appointed to this Division.'

delivered at Ahmedabad in 1958, also critically examined the working of the Planning Commission and made many suggestions for enhancing its usefulness. He admitted that the Commission had produced some technical reports of a high order but so far as its main job was concerned, it had not done it properly.

'The Planning Commission,' declared Professor Gadgil, 'has failed in almost every respect.' He added,

'It has failed to put together meaningful plans after due technical and other examination; it has failed to produce objective criteria relating to composition of programmes, allocations, etc.; it has failed to produce annual plans with appropriate breakdowns and failed to watch the progress of the Plan even in its broadest elements; it has failed to advise consistently on right policies being followed and at times even persisted in the adoption of wrong and inappropriate ones.'

Professor Gadgil felt that the situation could be remedied only by going back to the functions of the Planning Commission as originally laid down. It should not have executive powers and should not be mixed up with the essentially political process of policy making. The final decisions regarding economic policy should fully rest with the special Committees of the Cabinet and appropriate Committees of Secretaries, and ultimately the Cabinet itself. He also suggested that no minister including the Prime Minister should be a member of the Commission. If, however, the Cabinet should have a Minister for Planning, he alone should be a member of the Commission and its Chairman. The Deputy Chairman of the Commission should be 'an administrator of wide experience,' and other members should be experts, the expertize chiefly required being of natural scientists, technicians, social scientists, statisticians and economists.

Both the Estimates Committee and Professor Gadgil made their comments in 1958. Since then the composition and functions of the Commission have broadly remained the same, that is to say, Cabinet ministers still retain their membership of the Commission and it continues to exercise, as before, executive functions.[1]

[1] The formation of the National Planning Council by Lal Bahadur Shastri is discussed in chapter XI.

An important change that has been brought about in its composition is the appointment in November 1963 of Asoka Mehta as its Deputy Chairman. Mehta is widely respected for his ability and scholarship, but he lacks administrative experience which is very essential for one holding this key post in the Commission.

NATIONAL DEVELOPMENT COUNCIL

Apart from the Planning Commission, there is another body, namely, the National Development Council which is concerned with the formulation of economic policies. The Council was set up in August 1952 with a view to providing an opportunity to the State Governments to participate actively in the formulation of plans. 'In a country of the size of India,' said the Planning Commission, 'where the States have under the Constitution full autonomy within their own sphere of duties, it is necessary to have a forum such as a National Development Council at which, from time to time, the Prime Minister of India and the Chief Ministers of States, can review the working of the Plan and of its various aspects.'[1]

The functions of the National Development Council are:
(a) to review the working of the National Plan from time to time;
(b) to consider important questions of social and economic policies affecting national development; and
(c) to recommend measures for the achievement of the aims and targets set out in the National Plan, including measures to secure the active participation and co-operation of the people, improve the efficiency of the administrative services, ensure the fullest development of the less advanced regions and sections of the community and through sacrifices borne equally by all citizens, build up resources for national development.

The National Development Council consists of the Prime Minister, the Chief Ministers of all States and the Members of the Planning Commission.

According to V. T. Krishnamachari, the National Development Council has a 'vital role'. He observes:

[1] In January 1966, Ashok Mehta joined Mrs Gandhi's Cabinet as Minister for Planning while continuing as the Deputy Chairman of the Planning Commission.

'It provides a forum in which the Union Ministers and Chief Ministers of States discuss the Plans at important stages in their formulation. Plans are also approved at its meetings after their completion and before they are presented to the Parliament and the State Legislatures. In this way, the national character of the Plans is emphasized. The Council also considers social and economic policies affecting the country from a national point of view, so that where necessary uniformity may be secured. In these ways, it gives a lead to the country on broad issues of policy and promotes collective thinking and joint action on matters of national importance.'

But neither the Planning Commission nor the National Development Council has served as effective instruments of planning. The First Five Year Plan was carried out without much difficulty because it was relatively a modest Plan. It did not need large resources either from within or from abroad and, moreover, the favourable seasonal conditions helped to increase agricultural production. But the Second and Third Plans ran into serious difficulties. Production in agriculture and industry has shown no appreciable improvement. The foreign exchange situation has always remained critical owing to the large-scale import of food-grains and capital goods and the failure to bring about a substantial and continuous increase in exports. The inability to keep the prices of essential articles at reasonable levels has been causing concern particularly to the poorer sections of the community. Heavy taxation[1] has imposed a severe burden on the masses as well as on industries and has been an important factor in pushing up prices. At the same time, unemployment has become more acute than before. The Estimates Committee had suggested in 1958 that the unemployment problem should be tackled 'in a bold and energetic manner' and that there should be 'a continuous assessment of the progress made so that timely steps could be taken to ensure that the targets of employment laid down in the Second Plan are not only realized but even bettered to a substantial

[1] Against the target of additional taxation of Rs.1,750 crores indicated in the Third Plan, the Central and State Governments have already undertaken, in the first four years, taxation yielding about Rs.2,500 crores over the plan period.

degree.' The Second Plan, however, ended with a backlog of nine million unemployed; and the Third Plan mid-term apprai- sal, issued by the Planning Commission in November 1963, admitted that 'no serious dent has been made on the problem of unemployment'. The appraisal also pointed out that the annual rate of increase in national income in the two-year period 1961-3 was about 2·5 per cent as compared to the rate of over 5 per cent envisaged in the Third Plan.

In the circumstances, it is not surprising that the people have become disillusioned and the Planning Commission has been made the target of criticism. There is hardly any section of public opinion which has a good word to say about the achievements of the Commission. B. M. Birla, a leading industrialist, remarked in his speech at the annual meeting of the Federation of Indian Chambers of Commerce and Industry in March 1963 that we were planning for poverty and not for prosperity. He said:

'The Planning Commission says that even by 2000 A.D. one-third of the population will still be poor. What sort of planning is this? We have been planning since 1946 and will be planning up to 2000 A.D., that is for fifty-four years, and we shall still remain poor. If we have to remain poor, we could have remained poor even without planning. I think there is something very seriously wrong with our thinking.'

Nehru himself confessed that he had been rather frightened by the manner in which the Planning Commission had grown. He said in October 1963 : 'A close body of people, who think and advise Government, has grown into a huge organization with all the departments of Government almost duplicated there, and each one sending papers to the other. That is the normal habit of Government.'

The Commission was vigorously attacked by the Opposi- tion and also by members of the Congress Party during the debate in Parliament in November 1963 on the mid-term appraisal of the Third Plan. The Commission was described as 'a frustration squad' and its dilatory procedures were held respon- sible for the disappointing progress of the Plan. T. T. Krishna- machari, however, defended the Commission and commended its work in drawing up and supervising the implementations of the Plan. He said. 'It is not the Planning Commission's job to lay down policies or to implement the Plans. This is a sphere of responsibility essentially of the Government.' He added that the Commission was 'a useful weapon for by-passing the difficulties of a federal set-up. What the Central Ministers could not ask the States to do, the Planning Commission could.'[1]

While the dissatisfaction with the Planning Commission is understandable, the suggestions that it could be made more useful by depriving it of its executive functions and by excluding the Prime Minister and other ministers from its membership are hardly helpful. The critics seem to forget that if the plans have failed to deliver the goods, it is not due to the unwieldy nature of the Commission or its being a super-cabinet but precisely because planning has been done in an unrealistic and unscientific manner. There has been far too much of ideological bias in planning. In the name of socialism, whose objectives have never been clearly defined, the sphere of the State is being extended rapidly and activities have been undertaken which could very well have been left to the private sector. The bias in favour of heavy industries, fondness for huge and expensive projects, inadequate attention to minor irrigation, neglect of agriculture, excessive emphasis on austerity and curbs on consumption, failure to develop consumer industries vigorously and, above all, inefficiency in administration—it is these factors that have slowed down the progress of the economy and given a bad name to the Planning Commission. As Mr Tarlok Singh, a member of the Planning Commission, pointed out in a note circulated among members of the National Development Council in January 1965,

'The degree of discipline in policy, so essential for effective and continuous administrative action, has not been available in many key areas. This has been the position over the years, both at the

[1] In April 1964 the Planning Commission decided to divest itself of executive responsibility which it had taken upon itself in such fields as the rural works and industrialization programme, water supply and promotion of public co-operation in construction activities. Executive responsibility in these matters was transferred to the relevant Ministries. This did not mean, however, that the Commission would refrain from taking up and executing projects on its own.

national and state levels, and despite the existence of the National Development Council and several favourable political factors as between the Centre and the States.'

Certainly, the Commission needs to be overhauled. Its functions should be made advisory and its personnel recast. It should include not only eminent economists but also prominent industrialists whose practical experience will prove invaluable in the preparation and execution of the Plans.[1] But at the same time, the very techniques and objectives of planning should undergo a radical change so as to enthuse the people and create confidence in them that the Plans are meant to achieve prosperity here and now and not in a dim, distant future.

[1] This was sought to be done by the appointment of the National Planning Council referred to in chapter XI.

CHAPTER IX

HOW MANY MINISTERS?

One of the delicate tasks which the Prime Minister in a demo-cracy has to tackle is to determine the size of the Cabinet. There can, of course, be no rigid rules in this regard. The Prime Minister has to take into account various factors—personal, political, financial and administrative—in deciding about the number of colleagues he should have. The need to give representation to important regions is another major consideration. Regional fac-tors have played an important part in the selection of ministers in other countries as well. As Byrum E. Carter says, 'Regional representation has always been one of the considerations which the American President recognized in the formation of the Cabinet. Even those Presidents, whose Cabinets have been pre-dominantly from one section, must consider the wisdom of such action. Similarly in Canada, regional considerations are of the first importance . . . Although geographical considerations have some place in Britain, they are not of comparable importance to the position they occupy in the United States or Canada.'

Political writers in ancient India gave much thought to the size of the King's Cabinet. Authorities on Hindu Law generally favoured cabinets ranging from a strength of twelve to twenty. Kautilya did not suggest any specific number but he felt that the king should have an inner council of three or four ministers for frequent consultation on important and confidential matters, apart from other ministers whose advice he might seek occasion-ally. Akbar carried on with four principal ministers and Shivaji with eight.

Under the British rule, the Executive Council of Warren Hastings, the first Governor-General, had four members. Pitt's India Act of 1784 reduced it to three and the Council's strength remained at that figure till 1833 when a fourth member was added. A fifth member was appointed in 1861 and a sixth one in 1874. The Act of 1919 removed the statutory limitation on the strength of the Council and it was left to the discretion of the Governor-General to fix the number. The Council's strength in the subsequent years varied from time to time but it always remained a small and compact body. In 1939 it had seven members. Three years later, its strength was increased to fifteen and it remained at about this number until the interim government was set up in September 1946.

In the United Kingdom the Cabinets of the nineteenth century were relatively small in size. Robert Peel in 1841 had a Cabinet of fourteen and Disraeli had twelve. Henry Campbell-Bannerman in 1906 had a Cabinet of nineteen while Baldwin in 1935 had twenty-two. Attlee's Cabinet consisted of eighteen ministers while Churchill's of 1951 had sixteen. Macmillan's Cabinet had a strength of twenty-one. His successor Sir Alec Douglas-Home enlarged it to twenty-three which, according to *The Economist,* is 'at least five bigger than it ought to be for efficient functioning.' Wilson's Cabinet also contains twenty-three Ministers.

The consensus of opinion in the UK seems to favour a strength of not more than twenty. Attlee has suggested that the 'right size' of the Cabinet should be 'at the most sixteen,' while L. S. Amery feels that the ideal Cabinet should have about half a dozen ministers, all entirely free from departmental duties.

Small Cabinets have many advantages over larger ones. Apart from the merit of economy, small Cabinets are more convenient to manage; decisions can be reached more quickly; co-ordination is facilitated; secrecy is easier to maintain; and discipline and teamwork can be enforced more effectively.

Despite these advantages, however, it has not been possible for many countries to keep their Cabinets small because the functions of government have enormously increased in recent years. Besides, representation has to be given in the Cabinet, for political reasons, to influential groups within the party in power and so more ministers have to be appointed than what is strictly necessary.

The Indian Constitution does not provide for any specific number of Ministers either at the Centre or in the States. It is left to the discretion of the Prime Minister or the Chief Minister to determine the size of his Cabinet. This has also been the practice in Britain and many other democratic countries. As *The Economist* remarked, 'the Cabinet—down to and including Mr Wilson's—remains a pretty messy affair, rather too large and formed on no Platonic principles; its size and nature are determined by the interaction of the Prime Minister's wishes and of the pressures on him.'[1]

The Council of Ministers in free India was comparatively a small body in the beginning. Until the inauguration of the Republic in January 1950, there were fourteen Cabinet Ministers, four Ministers of State and two Deputy Ministers. After the general election in 1957, the Council consisted of thirteen Cabinet Ministers, fourteen Ministers of State and twelve Deputy Ministers. When the Cabinet was reconstituted after the general election in April 1962, it included seventeen Ministers of the Cabinet, twelve Ministers of State and twenty-two Deputy Ministers.

Nehru was often criticized for keeping large and unwieldy Cabinets. The criticism became more persistent soon after the proclamation of the emergency in October 1962. Many felt both in Parliament and outside that the Cabinet was too big to function effectively, especially when the country was confronted with the task of defending its integrity and independence against the Chinese attack. In the Lok Sabha a resolution was moved in November 1962 suggesting a reduction in the size of the Council of Ministers and emphasizing the need for rigorous austerity in ministerial circles. Nehru opposed the resolution, pointing out that the emergency had actually increased the work of the ministers. He said, 'merely to say that the Ministry should be reduced has no meaning to me. If the work is greater, it has to be done efficiently.'

STATES EMULATE CENTRE

One undesirable result of maintaining an unwieldy Cabinet at the Centre has been that the Chief Ministers of States also followed Nehru's example. Thus after the general election of 1962 States vied with one another in having the largest number of

[1] *The Economist* made these comments in its issue of February 13, 1965, while reviewing the book *Cabinet Reform in Britain 1914-1963* by Hans Daalder (Oxford).

ministers. The Punjab had thirty-one ministers as compared to fifteen in 1957. Uttar Pradesh increased its strength from nine to seventeen, Rajasthan from eleven to twenty and Assam from eight to fifteen. In addition, most States also maintained a large number of ministers of State, deputy ministers and parliamentary secretaries.

The Chief Minister of the Punjab, Sardar Pratap Singh Kairon, sought to justify the size of his Cabinet on the ground that it was necessary to establish the widest possible contact with the people and to understand their problems at first hand. The leaders of the opposition, he said, had been going about fostering regionalism among the people and telling them that their sectional interests were not fully safeguarded and, in order to counter their propaganda, representation had to be given in the Cabinet to the various sections. Further, a sum of Rs. 133 crores had to be spent in the execution of the Third Five Year Plan for the Punjab, and he wanted the largest team of men, imbued with a spirit of the Plan, to administer the funds for its effective implementation.

However, towards the end of 1962, the Punjab drastically cut down the size of its ministry to eight. This resulted in pressure being put on the Chief Ministers of other States to reduce the size of their ministry. But no Chief Minister was willing to follow the example of the Punjab on the ground that conditions in his State were fundamentally different.

The adoption of the Kamaraj Plan in September 1963 brought about a drastic reduction in Cabinet size both in the Centre and in the States. At the Centre the number of Cabinet ministers was reduced from eighteen to twelve and so far as the States were concerned, the Congress Parliamentary Board issued a directive to the effect that no State should have a ministry of more than twenty. This principle was generally followed in most States but an exception was made in regard to Uttar Pradesh and Maharashtra where the strength was permitted to be increased to twenty-one and twenty-five respectively.

Confining ourselves to the Centre, although in September 1963 the number of Cabinet ministers was reduced to eight under the Kamaraj Plan, it was increased in subsequent months; and with the appointment of Mahavir Tyagi as Minister of Rehabilitation in April 1964 its strength was raised to fourteen.[1] Moreover, the number of Ministers of State and Deputy Ministers was practically unaffected by the Kamaraj Plan. At the time of Nehru's death in May 1964, there were at the Centre fourteen Cabinet Ministers, twelve Ministers of State and twenty-one Deputy Ministers.

A large Cabinet is often sought to be justified in India on the ground of the vastness of the country. Even in the United Kingdom, which has only a population of about fifty-two million as compared with India's 450 million, the Council of Ministers under Harold Wilson consists of no fewer than 105 members— or roughly one Labour M.P. in three—including Cabinet Ministers, Ministers not in the Cabinet, Law Officers, Junior Ministers and Parliamentary Secretaries. But it should be remembered that the UK is a unitary State and India a federal one. In a federation, the Centre normally confines itself to those functions that are of national and strategic nature, leaving the rest to State Governments.

The large size of the Council of Ministers in India tends also to inflate administrative expenditure. Ministers are paid a monthly salary of Rs. 2,250 and Deputy Ministers Rs. 1,750/-. Cabinet Ministers, in addition, get a sumptuary allowance of Rs. 500 per month. The total expenditure on the salary and allowances of fifty-two ministers in 1962-3 was Rs. 21,61,000.[2] This, of course, is not a large sum, considering the fact that the Government of India's revenue expenditure is of the order of Rs. 2,000 crores per year. Even so, few will really cavil at the size or the expenditure on salary and allowances, provided the Council of Ministers as a whole works like a team with efficiency, determination and discipline in tackling the difficult problems confronting the country.[3]

[1] Tyagi was appointed Minister for Rehabilitation on April 16, 1964. April 16th has been a fateful day for Tyagi. He was appointed as Minister for Revenue on April 16, 1952. On April 16, 1956, he was transferred from the Finance Ministry to Defence. On April 16, 1957, he was dropped by Nehru in a ministerial reshuffle.

[2] In January 1965 the Lok Sabha rejected by 106 votes to ten H. V. Kamath's Salaries and Allowances of Ministers (Amendment) Bill. The Bill sought to raise the salary of Ministers from Rs.2,250 to Rs.2,500 per month and that of Deputy Ministers from Rs.1,750 to Rs.2,000; but it proposed to discontinue the present practice of giving them free furniture, electricity and water. It also sought to reduce the sumptuary allowance from Rs.500 per month to Rs.300.

[3] The strength of the Cabinet under Shastri and Mrs Gandhi is discussed in Chapters X and XII.

CHAPTER X

AFTER NEHRU—SHASTRI

Nehru died at about 2 p.m. on May 27, 1964, and immediately
G. L. Nanda, seniormost minister, was sworn in as the acting
Prime Minister. Some constitutional experts considered the
appointment of the acting Prime Minister as irregular and un-
necessary. The Indian Constitution contains no specific provision
for automatic succession when the Prime Minister dies in office.
It was, therefore, suggested that, as in Britain,[1] the President
should have asked the Council of Ministers to continue in office
until a new leader was elected and sworn in as Prime Minister.
Other experts, however, pointed out that with the death of the
Prime Minister, the Council stood dissolved. They referred to
Article 74(1) of the Constitution which clearly says that 'there
shall be a Council of Ministers with the Prime Minister at the
head to aid and advise the President in his functions.' And since
there cannot be a Council of Ministers without a Prime Minister,
the President did the right thing in asking Nanda to act until the
election of a new leader.

There is no doubt that, from the point of view of the spirit of
the Constitution, the procedure adopted by Radhakrishnan was
correct and democratic.

The choice of a successor to Nehru was the most difficult and
delicate task that ever confronted the Congress Party in its history of eighty-five years. Although the question, 'Who After
Nehru?' had been discussed all over the world for a long time,
few in the Congress took it seriously for, until the beginning of
1964, Nehru was in the best of health; and even when he fell ill
in January that year, he recovered quickly (though not completely) and was attending to his work as usual. In fact, in his
Press Conference on May 18th, when a correspondent raised the
succession issue, Nehru replied, 'My life is not going to end so

---

[1] According to A. B. Keith, 'Should the Prime Minister die in office, the rest
of the Ministers remain in office until the new Government is constituted.'

soon'; a remark that was greeted with loud applause by the Press-men, a rather unusual thing in a Press Conference. Nehru had also planned to attend the Commonwealth Prime Ministers' Con-ference in London in July 1964. His death, therefore, came as a complete surprise. It was all the more creditable, then, that the Congress was able to settle the succession problem swiftly and smoothly by unanimously electing Lal Bahadur Shastri as Prime Minister.

Certain aspects of the election deserve careful notice. Although technically it was the responsibility of the Congress Parliamen-tary Party to choose a new leader in place of Nehru, the Congress Working Committee also claimed a say in the matter because, it was argued, the future of the Congress organization itself would depend largely on how the new Prime Minister conducted the affairs of the nation.

TWO CONTESTANTS

There were actually two contestants—Morarji Desai and Lal Bahadur Shastri. Desai claimed the right to stand for the high office on the ground of his long and distinguished service to the Congress and the country. He had served as Chief Minister of Bombay with great ability; and as Union Minister of Commerce and Industry and as Finance Minister, he displayed considerable initiative and courage. He had been the seniormost minister of the Union Cabinet until his resignation in August 1963 under the Kamaraj Plan. Desai felt that had he continued in the Cabinet he, not Nanda, would have been made the acting Prime Minister and his claim to be Nehru's successor would have been unassail-able. He had submitted his resignation solely in the interest of party discipline and he expected that the Congress would recog-nize his services by electing him the Prime Minister.

Desai had a considerable following among States in the northern and eastern parts of India. He also received strong and unexpected support from the leftist group of the Congress led by Krishna Menon and K. D. Malaviya. These leaders, it was repor-ted, opposed the election of Shastri as Prime Minister because of his role in ousting them from Nehru's Cabinet. But Shastri was favoured by a majority of States, especially from the South.

Kamaraj, the Congress President and powerful provincial chiefs like Atulya Ghosh of West Bengal and Sanjiva Reddy of Andhra Pradesh also indicated their preference for Shastri. Those who backed Shastri found him to be the fittest successor to Nehru because, apart from his popularity and long political and parliamentary career, he was a man of moderate views, held in high esteem even by the parties in opposition. Moreover, it was widely believed that Nehru himself had unmistakably shown his liking for Shastri as his successor. After the death of Pandit Pant in 1961, Shastri became the Minister for Home Affairs, and in this capacity he did outstanding work that greatly endeared him to Nehru. The latter was also reportedly very reluctant to permit him to resign under the Kamaraj Plan. And so when, in January 1964, Nehru fell ill at Bhubaneswar he decided to take back into the Cabinet only Shastri in preference to senior leaders like Morarji Desai or Jagjivan Ram or S. K. Patil.

It now looked as if an open contest was inevitable and the Congress would split. At this stage the Congress Working Committee decided that the Congress should first ascertain the consensus among the Congress M.P.s and other members of the Party. Kamaraj, the Congress President, did this job with speed and adroitness, ably assisted by Atulya Ghosh of West Bengal, Sanjiva Reddy of Andhra Pradesh and Nijalingappa of Mysore. When Desai was informed that the consensus was overwhelmingly in favour of Shastri, he withdrew from the contest. So the Congress Parliamentary Party met in New Delhi on June 2nd, for the formal election of the new leader. Kamaraj presided over the meeting. Nanda, the acting Prime Minister, proposed the name of Shastri and it was promptly seconded by Desai, a gesture that greatly enhanced his reputation. Shastri was thus unanimously elected leader of the Congress Parliamentary Party.

Although the meeting was expected to be a mere formal affair, it was much more than that. As the Parliamentary Correspondent of the *Statesman* observed: 'It proved to be a historic occasion, as dramatic as it was dignified. It was solemn, somewhat poignant, and at times touching. Never before have so many Congress M.P.s—and Congress leaders who are not in Parliament —gathered under one roof as they did today under the domed central hall of Parliament House and seldom before have they been so conscious of history in the making as they were this morning.'

Why did Morarji Desai lose the contest? As we have seen, he had very good qualifications to be Prime Minister. But he had become rather unpopular when, in his capacity as Finance Minister—he held this key post continuously for five years—he introduced the Gold Control Bill and the compulsory deposit scheme for raising additional funds for fighting the Chinese aggression. Although the Cabinet fully supported these measures, they were looked upon as his creation and he was singled out for criticism. Desai's generally stubborn attitude also cost him some popularity. For example, in April 1963 when a demand was made in the Lok Sabha that the Attorney-General be summoned to the House to give his legal opinion on the compulsory deposit scheme, Desai, the then Finance Minister, declared bluntly that he would not agree to this suggestion 'even if that be the unanimous wish of the House.' This remark is believed to have irritated many Members of Parliament and ultimately led to his defeat in the battle of succession.

It is often suggested that Nehru himself never favoured the idea of Morarji Desai succeeding him as Prime Minister. D. R. Mankekar says, in his biography of Lal Bahadur Shastri, that Nehru took the decision to deny the leadership after him to Desai even as far back as 1961 when, after Pant's death, he blocked his formal promotion and designation as Number Two in the Cabinet. Mankekar observes:

'Nehru would appear to have convinced himself that democratic socialism, as also his other domestic and international policies, were not safe in Morarji's hands. Nehru considered Morarji's mind too narrow, rigid, closed and intolerant, apart from his much talked of rightist ideology. Nehru also thought Morarji did not possess the cohesiveness and tact needed to carry the entire party with him in the stormy days ahead.'

But, in my opinion, Nehru did not like Morarji Desai mainly because he found the latter to be a really competent man with a mind of his own. Nehru, like Winston Churchill, Franklin Roosevelt and many other great leaders, was fond of power, and if only if he had been in good health, he might have continued in office for another five-year term from 1967 after the fourth general election, and thereby established a unique record as Prime Minister for an unbroken period of nearly a quarter century. Of Churchill it has been said,

'No one who has really studied Churchill can honestly say that he enjoys being out of office. Every one of the relatively few years he has spent out of office, in the course of his long political life, he has hated. Every hour he has dreamed of the time when he could return, once more, to a position of power and authority.'[1]

Herbert Morrison relates an interesting anecdote about Roosevelt. Once when Morrison asked him during his first term of office as American President whether he would be standing for a second term, he replied, 'Morrison, being President of the United States is a terrible job. I am, so to speak, King, Prime Minister and party leader in a very big country. It is a hard, a very hard life. Who would want a second term?' Nevertheless, says Morrison, Roosevelt had a second term and indeed a third, and began a fourth before his much deplored death in 1945.[2] It is not surprising therefore if Nehru, in his anxiety to retain power, was unwilling to allow 'rivals near the throne'. Indeed, critics are not wholly wrong when they suggest that Nehru used the Kamaraj Plan to remove from the Cabinet certain colleagues whose presence had proved embarrassing to him.

SHASTRI'S REMARKABLE CAREER

What sort of man was Nehru's successor? He was a short, shy, simple and sincere man. He did not have the glamour and greatness of Nehru. India's first Prime Minister had become a world figure even before he took over that high office in August 1947. But Shastri was practically unknown outside India at the time of his election as Prime Minister. He had never been overseas. Nepal was the only foreign country he had visited. Nevertheless Shastri's career had been really remarkable.

[1] *Churchill by his Contemporaries,* edited by Charles Eade (Hutchinson).
[2] *Government and Parliament* by Herbert Morrison (Oxford).

Lal Bahadur Srivastava was born on October 2, 1904 in a poor family in Benaras. Having lost his father while still an infant, he had considerable difficulty in pursuing his education. His studies were interrupted in 1921 when he took an active part in Gandhian politics. But after a short while, he joined the Kasi Vidyapeeth, a nationalist institution run by well-known scholars like Dr Bhagavandas and Acharya Narendra Dev; and after a study for four years he took the degree of Shastri[1] in philosophy in the first division. Shastri thereafter became a life-member of the Servants of the People Society founded by Lala Lajpat Rai. This society, like the more famous Servants of India Society started by the great Gopal Krishna Gokhale in 1905, was established to train a band of young men who would work enthusiastically and unselfishly for the uplift of the poor and for the development of the country in every sphere. Membership of the Society gave Shastri opportunities to come into close contact with the masses and study their needs and aspirations. Shastri also actively participated in the civil disobedience movement which landed him in jail on several occasions. He had spent a total of nine years in jail and he devoted most of his time there to reading books on politics and philosophy.

Shastri and Nehru worked together closely in the Congress in many capacities. Among the important offices held by him in the Congress organization in the thirties were those of Secretary and President of the District and City Congress Committees at Allahabad, and General Secretary of the United Provinces Congress Committee.[2] Shastri's membership of the Allahabad Municipal Board for seven years and the Allahabad Improvement Trust for four years also helped him to acquire considerable practical experience in handling public affairs, which stood him in good stead in his ministerial career.

Unlike Nehru, Shastri came to his high office with vast parliamentary and administrative experience. After serving for some time as Parliamentary Secretary to Pandit Gobind Ballabh Pant,

[1] After joining politics, Lal Bahadur gave up his appellation 'Srivastava' which indicated his caste. 'Shastri' was not part of his name. It referred to the degree he got at Kasi Vidyapeeth. The Prime Minister signed his name as Lal Bahadur.
[2] In 1951 Shastri became General Secretary of the Indian National Congress under the presidency of Nehru.

the Chief Minister of Uttar Pradesh, Shastri was appointed in 1947 as Minister of Police and Transport in the same State. Five years later he joined Nehru's Cabinet as Minister for Railways and Transport in which capacity he did valuable work in improving the efficiency of railways—the largest undertaking in the public sector—and in providing more amenities to third class passengers. But two major accidents at short intervals shook the country's confidence in the railway administration. The first accident took place at Mehboobnagar in August 1956 in which 112 lives were lost; and three months later occurred another at Ariyalur in which 144 persons died. Shastri, the Minister in charge of railways, assumed moral responsibility for the disasters and resigned in November 1956.

Shastri, however, came back into the Cabinet in 1957 after the second general elections, in which he played an active part in achieving victory for the Congress. He was given the portfolio of Transport and Communications which he held for about a year. He then handled Commerce and Industry until April 1961 when he took over Home Affairs after the death of Pandit Pant. The fact that Nehru gave him this major assignment indicated the late Prime Minister's great confidence in his ability and integrity. During his tenure as Home Minister, the country was confronted with many grave problems such as language riots in Assam, threat of secession from the south, crisis in Kerala Congress, the Chinese invasion, and strained relations between New Delhi and Kathmandu; and in dealing with these issues, Shastri displayed firmness, tact and statesmanship and thereby created a good impression on the Prime Minister and the nation. It was therefore understandable that Nehru was unwilling to permit him to resign in August 1963 under the Kamaraj Plan. But, as we have seen, he was out of office only for about four months. He was recalled into the Cabinet in January 1964 and made Minister without Portfolio, in which capacity he worked till his election as Prime Minister in June 1964.

SHASTRI'S CABINET

Soon after he was elected Leader of the Congress Parliamentary Party, Lal Bahadur Shastri declared that a large Cabinet would be fully justified in view of the vastness of the country and the nature of the problems confronting it. But the Cabinet he formed in June 1964 was bigger by only two than what it was at the time of Nehru's death. Shastri's Cabinet in the beginning consisted of sixteen Ministers. In addition, there were fifteen Ministers of State and twenty Deputy Ministers. Of the Cabinet Ministers, seven were above sixty years of age, namely, Dasappa seventy, Nanda sixty-five, Krishnamachari sixty-five, Tyagi sixty-five, Patil sixty-four, Chagla sixty-four and Satyanarain Sinha sixty-four. Eight Ministers were below sixty, namely, Kabir fifty-eight, Swaran Singh fifty-seven, Subramaniam fifty-four, Sanjiva Reddy fifty-one, A. Sen fifty-one, Chavan fifty-one, Mrs. Gandhi forty-seven and Sanjivayya forty-three; Shastri himself was sixty.

Shastri retained most of the ministers who had worked under Nehru. There were only three new additions—Mrs Indira Gandhi, Sanjiva Reddy and S. K. Patil. Patil was already a member of the Lok Sabha. He was the Food Minister in Nehru's Cabinet from August 1959 until he resigned in August 1963. Mrs Gandhi and Sanjiva Reddy were not members of the Lok Sabha at the time of their appointment, but subsequently were elected to the Rajya Sabha.

The ranking of Ministers caused considerable embarrassment to the new Prime Minister. He was keen to bring Morarji Desai into the Cabinet not only because of his long ministerial experience but because he had gracefully agreed to permit him to be elected unopposed as the Prime Minister. But Desai insisted that he should get the second rank since he had held it previously under Nehru until his resignation under the Kamaraj Plan. He was not very particular about the portfolio that might be assigned to him but he was adamant in being ranked second. The second rank was held by Nanda; and he was equally keen to retain it because he had acted as Prime Minister for twelve days following Nehru's death. Shastri offered Desai the third rank but he rejected it. The third rank was held by Krishnamachari and the fourth by Mrs Indira Gandhi.

As regards the distribution of work, Shastri himself took over the portfolios formerly held by Nehru, namely, Foreign Affairs and Atomic Energy. He also assumed the Chairmanship of the

Planning Commission. Other important changes were the following: Swaran Singh was switched over from Food and Agriculture to Industry and Supply,[1] C. Subramaniam was transferred from Steel to Food and Agriculture and Sanjiva Reddy, a new entrant, was given Steel and Mines. H. C. Dasappa was shifted from Railways to Irrigation and Power which, in the last phase of Nehru's Premiership, was handled by a Minister of State. Patil was given Railways which Nehru had offered to him in 1963 and which he declined for reasons explained earlier. The other Cabinet Ministers were left undisturbed in charge of the portfolios they were holding under Nehru.

At the level of Minister of State, the only notable change (apart from reallocation of certain portfolios) was that the Minister for International Trade was designated Minister of Commerce, and cotton textiles, jute and sericulture were transferred back to this Ministry from the Ministry of Industry.

The number of Deputy Ministers was reduced from twenty-two to twenty, with some changes in their assignments.

However, within six weeks after the formation of the Cabinet, Shastri felt compelled, because of ill-health, to give up External Affairs. This portfolio was entrusted to Sardar Swaran Singh. This change was widely welcomed in the country because for the first time India had a whole-time Cabinet Minister to look after the important portfolio of External Affairs. Now the Prime Minister was able to devote more attention to domestic problems, particularly to the task of ensuring co-ordination among his colleagues. The choice of Swaran Singh was considered appropriate since he had travelled widely and played a leading role in many delicate negotiations between India and Pakistan as well as on certain other occasions. H. C. Dasappa was transferred to Industry and Supply and K. L. Rao, Minister of State, was given independent charge of Irrigation and Power, which he was holding under Nehru.

[1] The Economist, London, commented as follows on the new assignment for Swaran Singh: 'The most encouraging change, perhaps, is the replacement at the Food Ministry of Sardar Swaran Singh, whose considerable talents, while he held that post, were vigorously devoted to international affairs, by C. Subramaniam. Subramaniam was that rare thing, a successful Steel Minister. He might yet be that rarer thing, a successful Food Minister. India could certainly do with one.'

Shastri's Cabinet appeared more homogeneous than it was under Nehru. But the allocation of portfolios in some respects did not seem quite rational. For instance, the Minister of Law was given charge of subjects like village industries and welfare of backward classes. The Ministry of Petroleum and Chemicals dealt with the International Congress of Orientalists, revision of gazetteers and the Muslim Wakfs Act. The combination of Communications and Parliamentary Affairs also seemed rather incongruous. Besides, the way in which subjects relating to Commerce and Industry were split up and assigned to different persons was not conducive to maximum efficiency. For example, while steel was looked after by a Cabinet Minister, Industry and Heavy Engineering were assigned to a Minister of State. The Minister of Commerce was not given a place in the Cabinet though he dealt with a major assignment like export promotion which was of great importance to the economy. The allotment of portfolios seemed to have been done in some cases for satisfying the desires of individual ministers rather than from the point of administrative convenience or efficiency.

The most powerful and influential ministers in Shastri's Cabinet were Krishnamachari, Nanda, Patil, Mrs Gandhi and Sanjiva Reddy. They constituted the 'inner Cabinet'.[1] Krishnamachari's power arose from his deep knowledge of economic problems and the key portfolio of Finance which he handled with great ability. As Finance Minister he wielded considerable authority over other departments and over the Planning Commission. As Blake points out in his book, *The Unknown Prime Minister*, the office of the Chancellor of the Exchequer 'gives its holder great authority and power. There is none other except the Prime Ministership which gives such influence or starting point of influence when in right hands.' It was significant that when Shastri was unable to go to London to attend the Commonwealth Prime Ministers' Conference in July 1964, it was Krishnamachari who represented him and not Nanda although he was second in rank in the Cabinet. Krishnamachari, however, had to submit his resignation in

[1] The qualification for entry into the 'inner cabinet', says John P. Mackintosh, is not seniority, office, or ability, but possession of the Prime Minister's confidence.

December 1965 due to the circumstances which are explained in a subsequent paragraph.

Nanda, too, had considerable influence because, apart from his seniority which entitled him to preside over Cabinet meetings in the absence of the Prime Minister, he was in charge of the important department of Home Affairs. His crusade against corruption, though not spectacularly successful, had helped to enhance his reputation. S. K. Patil, a leader of all-India fame, was perhaps the ablest organizer, orator and parliamentarian in Shastri's Cabinet. Mrs Gandhi, although she lacked previous ministerial experience, commanded great prestige in the Congress and in the country. Her assignment, namely, Information and Broadcasting, was not important in terms of power but, significantly, she was given the fourth rank in the Cabinet, the same that Shastri had held since January 1964 until his election as Prime Minister.

The appointment of Sanjiva Reddy to the Cabinet created considerable surprise. He had, of course, political and ministerial experience. He was a Minister in the composite Madras State for two years and he became the first Chief Minister of Andhra Pradesh when that State came into existence in October 1956. He resigned this post in December 1959 on his election as President of the Indian National Congress. But he again became the Chief Minister of Andhra Pradesh in March 1962 and held that office till January 1964 when he resigned in deference to the Supreme Court judgment relating to the nationalization of bus routes in the Kurnool district. The Court had held that Reddy, as Chief Minister, had been motivated by 'bias and ill-will' against certain private operators whose bus routes had been nationalized by the Government of Andhra Pradesh. Reddy, moreover, was not a member of Parliament.

His appointment therefore came in for criticism both in the Lok Sabha and outside. A debate was held in the Lok Sabha in October 1964 in the course of which several members strongly objected to Reddy's appointment when the country's highest Court had passed an adverse verdict against him only a few months earlier. The Speaker, however, ruled:

'We are not here to decide who is to be appointed Minister or not. It is for the Prime Minister to appoint his Cabinet. It is for the Prime Minister to take into his Cabinet those persons who he thinks would suit or would be proper or would be honest . . . It is for him to decide and not for this House to decide. Once he is appointed, the only remedy that this House has got is that it might move a vote of no-confidence.'

It is believed that Reddy was chosen as a Minister because he had played, along with Kamaraj and other leaders, a crucial part in getting Shastri elected as Prime Minister; and this explained Reddy's influence in the Cabinet.

Shastri introduced some important changes in regard to the working of the Cabinet. In the first place, he set up his own Secretariat. Nehru too had his Secretariat to assist him but, according to K. Rangaswami, Political Correspondent of *The Hindu*, it was

'a kind of private office and it was not a Secretariat in the real sense of the term. It had never been the function of the former Prime Minister's Secretariat to keep abreast of events and draw the Prime Minister's attention to important developments in the country.'

Shastri's Secretariat however, was organized differently. Its main work was to keep the Prime Minister informed of major developments in India and abroad and their implications. It was headed by L. K. Jha, a senior ICS officer. There were also two Joint Secretaries, in addition to the other staff. The Cabinet Secretariat continued, as before, to deal with the co-ordination of work at the secretariat level. Anxiety was expressed in certain quarters that a full-fledged secretariat for the Prime Minister was likely to lead to friction and misunderstanding between him and his colleagues. But so long as Shastri remained as the Prime Minister there was no serious conflict.

The second major change introduced by Shastri was in the sphere of public relations. Cabinet decisions, which were not of a confidential nature, were released to the Press by the Cabinet Secretary at the end of every meeting. The proposal to inform the Press of Cabinet decisions was seriously considered by Nehru on several occasions. But he did not seem to favour it. Some idea of the reaction of the Press to Shastri's decision can be had from the report that appeared in *The Hindu* of August 18, 1964:

'The decisions taken by the Cabinet at its last two meetings were not particularly spectacular. One decision was about India's association with the international film liaison centre. Another relates to the setting up of a University in Delhi. A third was the appointment of a judge for some enquiry. The fact that some decisions are being announced should be welcomed ... But if the subjects on which decisions are reached should continue to be of the same character as were considered at the last two meetings, the people are bound to wonder whether a Cabinet meeting is at all necessary for dealing with such minor items and whether a Cabinet never considered other subjects of greater importance, national and international.'

The third change introduced by Shastri was to hold informal Cabinet meetings at the residence of each Cabinet Minister by rotation. The Prime Minister usually presided over such meetings.

CHAPTER XI

COURAGE AND CAUTION

In his Republic Day message to the nation in January 1965, Dr Radhakrishnan referred to the 'dignified and orderly transition' to the new leadership and said that Government which enjoyed popular support was functioning with 'courage and caution', However, not many were prepared to agree with this view of the President. In fact, critics complained that Shastri was displaying too much weakness and vacillation in handling the great issues confronting the nation. For instance, C. Rajagopalachari said in a meeting at Bombay on February 14, 1965, 'I had great hopes when Lal Bahadur Shastri took over the reins of power and I had congratulated him and prayed for his success. But I am sorry to say he has proved a disappointment.' The Swatantra leader's assessment, however, was rather unfair because by then Shastri had been in the saddle for only about six months and though on occasion he might have displayed a lack of firmness, he had also acted boldly in many instances and shown that he was a leader with a mind of his own. The world, however, knew of his great courage only in September 1965 when he ordered the troops to march into Pakistan territory to defend India's integrity. But it is necessary to point out that even before he took this momentous decision, he had given indications of bold leadership.

NO YIELDING TO PRESSURE

It is significant to recall that at the time of Shastri's election as Prime Minister, Kamaraj, the Congress President, made it clear that Nehru's death had created a big void in leadership and that none was competent to fill the gap. He said,

'It is impossible for anyone to fill the role of the great departed leader, and yet we have to shoulder the responsibility that has come to us. The responsibility cannot be discharged individually by anybody. It is by collective responsibility, collective leadership and collective approach alone we can undertake this great task before us.'

This statement created the impression that Shastri would be just one among equals in the Cabinet and that he would always have to act in consultation not only with his ministerial colleagues but also with the Congress President and other powerful leaders who had helped his election. In fact, it was even pointed out that in the choice of his Cabinet and the distribution of portfolios, Shastri had allowed himself to be unduly influenced by what has come to be called as the 'syndicate', that is, the Congress President and leaders like Atulya Ghosh who played a prominent part in the choice of the Prime Minister.[1]

But Shastri was prompt in scotching such rumours. In a statement in Nagpur on June 16, 1964 he said, 'I cannot effectively function as Prime Minister of India if I yield to any pressure in such matters. I will not yield to any pressure from any quarter.' Shastri also emphatically denied, in an interview with his biographer D. R. Mankekar, that he was being dictated to by various pressure groups. He said,

'I can say without any disrespect to any other colleague that I have not consulted a single person in so far as the formation of my Cabinet was concerned. Even additions and alterations were my own. In the matter of appointment of Ministers of my Government I have been secretive. With apologies to my colleagues, I want to keep this to myself in future also, if and when the occasion arises. It is but natural that I should take the whole responsibility for this on my shoulders.'[2]

According to Pran Chopra of the *Statesman*, Shastri attached

[1] Speaking at the West Bengal Congress Political Conference on March 13, 1965, N. Sanjiva Reddy, Union Minister for Steel and Mines, strongly denied the existence of a 'syndicate' in the Congress organization. He said, 'Shastri is the undisputed leader of the country. Neither I nor Atulya Ghosh has ever attempted to advise Shastri. What we have done is meant to strengthen the Prime Minister's hands. There is nothing like a syndicate. Only those who are angry for having been left out of the leadership are talking about a syndicate.'
[2] *Lal Bahadur: A Biography* by D. R. Mankekar (Popular Prakashan, Bombay).

the highest importance to integrity in the choice of his colleagues. In an interview he gave to Chopra in June 1964, Shastri revealed his anxiety to form a government that would inspire confidence among all sections of the people in ministerial incorruptibility. 'It is not,' says Chopra, 'that he suspected that there was much corruption to be rooted out, but he wanted a Government which would win the trust of the people even if it did not overawe them with its talent.'

Apart from the formation of the Cabinet, there were also other instances where Shastri took the decisions by himself. The most conspicuous example was in regard to the manufacture of the atom bomb. When early in October 1964, China exploded the bomb, Indian public opinion was greatly alarmed. The explosion was looked upon as a serious threat to the security of India. Till then it was believed that China was incapable of undertaking the manufacture of nuclear weapons because of her technical and economic backwardness and the huge expenditure involved. But when China did explode the bomb, it created an entirely new situation for India and for the world at large. It was feared that nuclear weapons in the hands of a ruthless and powerful country like China would pose a terrible threat to India's security. Public opinion in India reacted strongly and there was a persistent demand that the Government of India should immediately undertake the manufacture of atom bombs, irrespective of the costs involved, in order to meet effectively the Chinese challenge. This demand, of course, was not unanimous. Many thought that if India also entered the atomic race, it would not only be a negation of the principle of universal disarmament which she had consistently advocated, but it would also cripple her economic progress by diverting large sums from productive investment to the manufacture of nuclear weapons. Into the details of this debate, it is unnecessary to enter here. Naturally it was thought that so vital an issue would be carefully examined in all its aspects by the Cabinet. But it was not. As soon as the public discussion began, following the Chinese explosion, Shastri declared that it would not be in the interest of India to produce the bomb because it would be against the principles of Mahatma Gandhi and Jawaharlal Nehru. Indian resources were meagre and so the country could not afford to embark upon such a programme.

He suggested that the Chinese threat should be countered by intensifying the campaign against nuclear weapons. If international public opinion asserted itself emphatically and if the great powers like the USA, the UK and Russia could take the initiative in this matter and agree among themselves on measures to save the world from an atomic war, it would be difficult for China to carry out her nuclear threat.

Shastri went on reiterating this view for several weeks. But on November 23, 1964 he made the surprising disclosure that the Cabinet had not yet discussed the situation arising from the Chinese explosion of the atom bomb. Apparently, Shastri had thought that a Cabinet decision was unnecessary since in any case, from the practical point of view, India could not afford to make a sudden and fundamental change in her policy towards nuclear weapons. It is not known whether the Cabinet ever discussed the matter subsequently. But this example shows that Shastri was not always acting in consultation with the Cabinet.

FRIENDSHIP TOWARDS ALL

The record of Shastri's Cabinet could be considered broadly in terms of foreign affairs and domestic issues. In foreign affairs, the Government continued Nehru's policy of non-alignment and friendship with all nations. But Shastri tried to strengthen India's ties with the neighbouring countries to a greater extent than they were under Nehru. Shortly after his appointment as Minister of External Affairs, Swaran Singh undertook a tour of Nepal, Burma, Afghanistan, Ceylon and other Asian countries in order to bring about closer relationship between them and India. An agreement was concluded with Ceylon over the problem of Indian residents, which had defied solution for a number of years. Though the agreement did not help to protect effectively the interests of the people of Indian origin, it at least served to promote more cordial relations between India and Ceylon. India participated in the Conference of non-aligned nations held at Cairo in October 1964. Although it did not achieve much in terms of concrete results, it provided Shastri with his first opportunity to go overseas and meet the leading statesmen of Asia. Shastri created a good impression by his speech at the Conference although his suggestion that a peace mission be sent to China to persuade her to halt her programme of nuclear development fell flat. In making this proposal, Shastri had not consulted his Cabinet.

Shastri paid his first visit to England in December 1964 and established personal contact with Prime Minister Wilson and other Ministers of the British Government. His tour of Russia in May 1965, which lasted about seven days, was successful in strengthening the political and economic relationship between India and the Soviet Union. In the joint communique issued simultaneously in New Delhi and Moscow on May 19th Shastri and Kosygin, the Russian Prime Minister, reiterated their faith in peaceful co-existence and stressed the need for a radical improvement of the international situation, for eliminating the threat of a nuclear war, for the achievement of general and complete nuclear disarmament, and for the settlement of all international disputes, including border and territorial disputes, by friendly negotiations. The Soviet Union agreed to continue to give economic and technical assistance to India during the Fourth Five-Year Plan, particularly for constructing specific enterprises relating to iron and steel, non-ferrous metals, mining and oil industries, power supply and development of fishery. Russia also agreed to continue to train Indian personnel in higher technology. Both countries further expressed their desire to double Indo-Soviet trade by 1970 as compared to 1964; (Indian exports to Russia in 1964 were valued at Rs. 75.33 crores and imports from Russia amounted to Rs. 72.64 crores) and for this purpose, a trade agreement was concluded in January 1966.

While India's ties with Russia were thus strengthened, the relationship between New Delhi and Washington became somewhat strained as a result of President Johnson's request to Shastri to postpone his visit to the USA, scheduled in June 1965. The manner and timing of the President's request unfortunately seemed to create the impression that the USA was trying to express its displeasure at India's action in criticizing American policy in Vietnam. However, this setback in Indo-US friendship was only a passing phase and once again the world's two largest democracies resumed their cordial relations as in the past.

Shastri visited Canada in June 1965 and created a profound

impression there.[1] Canada had been offering substantial assistance to India for developing atomic energy and for other purposes; and as a result of Shastri's visit, the political and economic ties between the two countries became closer. In the same month, Shastri played a prominent part in the Commonwealth Prime Ministers' Conference in London. He made a constructive contribution to the discussions at the Conference on major issues particularly those relating to Vietnam and Southern Rhodesia.

Although Shastri succeeded in maintaining the friendship of the Western bloc and the Communist bloc, thereby getting substantial aid from both, his efforts to promote amity with Pakistan did not meet with immediate success. From time to time, there were many incidents on the Indo-Pakistani border which often led to loss of lives on both sides and created tension between the two countries. The dispute over the Rann of Kutch in May-June 1965 took a violent turn and at one time it looked as if it would break out into a major war. But this problem was amicably settled through the initiative and goodwill of Prime Minister Wilson.

CABINET AND THE KASHMIR WAR

The Indo-Pakistani agreement on the Kutch-Sind border signed on June 30, 1965 was expected to reduce tension and promote friendship between the two countries. But this hope did not materialize. Pakistan tried to annex Kashmir by force by instigating armed infiltrators to undermine the morale of the people and sabotage strategic sectors of the State, and by launching, on September 1st, an open attack by its regular forces in the Chhamb sector on the Indian territory. India then had no alternative but to fight back and so, on September 6th, the Indian Army crossed the Punjab border in the Lahore sector. This intensified the conflict. There was no formal declaration of war and the two countries

[1] Claude Ryan, Editor of Le Devoir, a leading French newspaper of Canada, wrote thus of Shastri after an interview: 'Physically small and lean, he hardly looks a Prime Minister and so unassuming that looking at him one gets a feeling that he needs help. When talking he takes no advantage of his position as head of one of the most important and popular countries of the world. He weighs his words, meditates on a point before replying and replies to a question as if he is embarrassed by the question. He speaks in a slightly subdued voice and never raising the tone most of the time he contents himself to stating facts without any ideology.'

continued to maintain diplomatic relations. Nevertheless, it was practically a regular war in which both sides fought each other fiercely, resulting in considerable damage and destruction to both. The fighting came to an end on September 22, 1965 through the intervention of the United Nations.

What was the impact of the war on the Government of India and the nation? In the first place, the war greatly enhanced the reputation of Shastri. His decision in ordering the Indian forces to march into Pakistani territory to repel aggression was hailed throughout the country. It was felt that in the then circumstances there was no other course open to India to save her honour, freedom and integrity. Till then, the people in India and abroad had thought of Shastri as a mild man, perhaps good enough for leading the people in times of peace, but unsuited to handle a grave crisis. But Shastri's decision revealed to the world that Nehru's successor was by no means a 'soft' man, wedded to non-violence at all costs but a great leader of courage and realism.

Secondly, the war created remarkable solidarity among the people. Political, religious and linguistic differences were buried for the time being and the nation rose as one man to defend its freedom.

Thirdly, the war brought about greater unity within the Cabinet, and between the Cabinet and Parliament. Shastri took care to see that, as far as possible, major decisions during the war were taken in consultation not only with the Cabinet but also with the leaders of the Opposition. The Emergency Committee of the Cabinet was enlarged by including C. Subramaniam, the Food Minister, S. K. Patil, the Minister for Railways, and N. Sanjiva Reddy, the Minister for Steel. The meetings of the Emergency Committee were also attended by the top civilian and military advisers. Besides, the Prime Minister held frequent consultations with the President of India as well as the Congress President. To what extent Shastri had won over his political opponents will be clear from the fact that, after the proclamation of the cease-fire on September 22, 1965, Opposition members in the Lok Sabha vied with one another in paying their tribute to the Prime Minister for his bold leadership. Shastri said,

'I have heard from every side of the House only one voice, the voice of patriotism, of common will to defend the sovereignty and territorial integrity of India, no matter who the invader may be. This is the voice of the people of India, expressed in unmistakable terms, through their chosen representatives in Parliament. In fact, it is this unity which has been the biggest source of strength to all of us in these testing times. I am grateful to the House for the magnificent support given during these historic times.'

Unfortunately, however, after the cease-fire the Cabinet once again seemed to display a lack of unity and discipline. This was revealed by C. Subramaniam, Food Minister, at a symposium organized by the Central Board of Irrigation and Power in New Delhi on November 6, 1965. He said that unless the rigid boundaries between the Union Ministries, that were sovereign empires in themselves, were pulled down and a team spirit created in the administration, there would be no salvation for this country. 'Each of us is jealous of his empire and does not quite welcome others taking a peep into it,' he said. Subramaniam felt that these empires must vanish, the boundary walls must fall, and a free flow of plans and ideas must take place to ensure correct administration for a big, problem-ridden country like ours.'[1]

THE CABINET AND THE ECONOMY

The Indo-Pakistani war also greatly disrupted India's economic progress; and in order to understand its impact, it is necessary to trace briefly how Shastri's Cabinet handled the economic situation.

When Shastri took over as Prime Minister, the economic condition of the country was far from satisfactory. The Third Five-Year Plan had run into serious difficulties. The Plan had expected that the national income at constant prices would increase by about five per cent per year. But in the first three years of the Plan (1961-2 and 1963-4), it had increased by not more than three per cent per annum. At the same time, the population had

[1] T. T. Krishnamachari's statement on his resignation in December 1965 also indicated clearly that the Indo-Pakistan war did not produce a wholesome effect on Cabinet solidarity. This is explained in chapter XI.

grown by more than two per cent per year. There was therefore, hardly any real improvement in the living standards of the people. The slow growth of the economy was mainly due to the stagnation in agricultural production. Agriculture contributes nearly fifty per cent to the national income. But, despite its crucial importance, it had not received the attention it deserved. The production of foodgrains had been of the order of eighty million tonnes in the first three years of the Plan and, at this rate, the Plan's target of 100 million tonnes was most unlikely to be achieved by 1965-66. The failure to grow sufficient food was due to several causes such as unfavourable weather, lack of efficient administration, inadequate supply of fertilisers, superior seeds, water and pesticides, and a land policy that created a large number of uneconomic holdings.

Industrial production too had failed to record a continuous increase. The Third Plan had expected industrial production to rise by about eleven per cent per year but, in the first three years, it had not increased by more than seven or eight per cent. The slow rate of growth was mainly due to the acute scarcity of foreign exchange which led to the shortage of imported raw materials and components. The supply of indigenous materials like coal and cement was also not adequate and regular. Moreover, the high level of personal and corporate taxation, frequent changes in fiscal policy and the fixation of unremunerative prices for several industries like steel, coal, cement, sugar and paper impeded a steady increase in production. The capital market had been in a depressed condition ever since the beginning of 1962. Established companies were finding it difficult to raise funds for expansion and modernization while the promoters of new companies were faced with poor response from the investing public. The total capital raised by non-Government companies was only Rs. 80 crores in 1963 while it was Rs. 105 crores in 1962 and about Rs. 100 crores in 1961. The situation showed no appreciable improvement in 1964. The Government had given more importance to heavy industries that involved huge investment and long gestation periods. The industries producing consumer goods did not get the priority and the importance due to them, considering their vital role in fighting the inflationary tendencies.

It was not surprising therefore that the prices of foodgrains and other essential commodities had caused a sharp increase, resulting in great distress to the large majority of the people. While some increase in prices was inevitable in a developing economy, the steep and sudden rise created a very difficult problem. In the six months April-September 1963 the price level of all commodities rose by fifteen per cent or by an average of 2·5 per cent per month. As the Federation of Indian Chambers of Commerce and Industry remarked,

'The whole economic situation now presents a rather confused picture of imbalance and contrary movements. Production is falling all along the line or increasing at a lower rate than planned. Commodity prices have been rising while share prices have been falling. Taxation has reached a point at which no investible funds are forthcoming.'

Thus the Shastri Cabinet was faced with a critical situation. It was therefore decided to adjust economic policy with a view to giving greater emphasis to consumer goods industries, improvement in agricultural production in the short period, revival of activity in the capital market, promotion of efficiency in the public sector undertakings, greater financial and monetary discipline, vigorous expansion of exports, more rigid control of imports, and better arrangements for the distribution of essential commodities. The food problem was tackled mainly by importing substantially larger quantities of rice and wheat than in the previous years. The quantity of foodgrains imported in 1964 was 6·27 million tonnes as compared to 4·56 million tonnes in 1963 and 3·64 million tonnes in 1962. Other measures to improve the food situation included the provision of more fertilizers to cultivators, larger releases from Government stocks, extension of fair price shops, and fixation of maximum foodgrain prices at the wholesale and retail level. The Food Corporation was set up to undertake trading in foodgrains in a commercial manner, to ensure that the primary producer obtained the minimum price that might be announced from time to time, and to protect the consumer from the vagaries of speculative trade.

For stimulating industrial growth, the price control in respect of certain commodities was relaxed, and the procedures for licensing new industrial units were somewhat liberalized. An important change was adopted in the policy towards foreign capital. Hitherto 'letters of intent' were issued only to Indian industrialists who wished to enter into collaboration arrangements with their counterparts in foreign countries. But it was decided towards the end of 1964 to issue such letters to prospective private foreign investors who wanted to establish joint ventures in India. The Government hoped that this procedure would help to attract more private capital from abroad and expedite the programme of industrial development. Steps were also taken to strengthen the institutional arrangements for providing loan finance to private industries. The Unit Trust was set up for mobilizing the people's savings and for providing equity capital to industry. Another important measure was the introduction in December 1964 of a scheme to encourage the flow of funds from individuals for investment in new equities. Under this scheme, investments up to certain sums in equity shares of new companies would be entitled to tax credit certificates for a period of four years. It was expected that this concession would help to compensate shareholders for the long period they would have to wait for the companies to achieve full production and declare dividends.

These measures however did not bring about any substantial improvement in the Indian economy. The fact was that due to heavy taxation on individuals and corporations, there was no adequate incentive or opportunity for established industries to expand or for new companies to come into existence. The capital market continued to be in a depressed condition and a large proportion of the amounts raised by new equity issues had to be subscribed by underwriters. Industrialists, and businessmen in general, lacked enthusiasm and confidence in the future of the economy. 'I have been in business for over forty years but never have I seen such universal gloom among businessmen,' declared J. R. D. Tata, a well-known industrialist, in his speech at the meeting of the Central Advisory Council of Industries held in New Delhi towards the end of January 1965. That summed up, in brief, the view of India's business community regarding the handling of economic affairs by the Cabinet.

The Union Budget for 1965-66, presented to Parliament on

February 27, 1965 attempted to improve the situation by lowering the incidence of indirect taxes, by cutting down the level of personal taxation and by providing certain incentives to the corporate sector. The excise duty on many articles of common consumption such as cotton cloth, footwear, writing and printing paper, vegetable products, cycle tyres and tubes and cycle parts, was either reduced or removed. The tax on personal incomes was reduced on all levels. The highest marginal rate on unearned income was lowered from 88·125 per cent to 82·5 per cent and on earned income from 82·5 per cent to 74·75 per cent. Some relief was provided to companies also. It was laid down that a ceiling would be fixed to the income-tax, including the tax charged with reference to distribution of equity dividends, and surtax at seventy per cent of the total income of companies. The Government also took powers to issue tax credit certificates to companies with a view to encouraging production and exports.

The budget proposals were, on the whole, welcomed by industry and trade. Nevertheless, there was keen disappointment that the reliefs granted to individuals and companies were very meagre and quite inadequate to stimulate industrial expansion in a big way. The burden of taxation continued to be heavy. The Finance Minister himself admitted in his budget speech that despite the reduction he had effected, 'our tax rates will still be higher than in countries like the United Kingdom and the United States of America at corresponding levels of income.'[1]

A major task that the Shastri Cabinet had to perform in the economic sphere was the preparation of the Fourth Five-Year Plan that would be in operation from 1966-7 to 1970-71. Although the formulation of the details was the work of the Planning Commission, it was the responsibility of the Cabinet to ensure that the Plan was drawn up realistically so that it could be implemented without much difficulty. The memorandum prepared by the Planning Commission proposed an outlay of Rs. 21,500 crores to Rs. 22,500 crores, the actual figure to be determined upon a re-assessment of resources at a later stage.

The reception to the Fourth Plan memorandum in the country, however, was not uniform. While all were agreed on the need to

[1] On August 19, 1965, Krishnamachari, the Finance Minister, presented a mid-term budget, which imposed fresh taxation of about Rs. 176 crores.

accelerate the development of the economy, opinion was divided as to how exactly it was to be done. The private industrial sector, for instance, felt that when the country was not able to implement successfully the Third Plan with an outlay of only Rs. 11,600 crores, it would be difficult to carry through a Plan costing around Rs. 22,000 crores. The Third Plan, it was feared, would end with shortfalls in many major fields. The production of foodgrains by 1965-6 (the last year of the Third Plan) was expected to be only ninety-two million tonnes against the target of 100 million tonnes. The output of steel ingots would be not more than seven million tonnes against the target of over nine million tonnes. The production of machine tools would not be more than Rs. 25 crores as compared to the target of Rs. 30 crores. For mill-made cloth the target was 5,800 million yards but production was estimated at 5,300 million yards. The shortfalls in fertilizers would be substantial : the target was 800,000 tonnes in terms of nitrogen against which the production was expected to be about 425,000 tonnes.

Anxiety about the feasibility of the Fourth Plan in its present form was expressed also by the Congress President K. Kamaraj. In his presidential address at the annual session of the Congress held at Durgapur in January 1965, Kamraj suggested that the Government of India and the Planning Commission should carefully examine the implications of the Fourth Plan because 'any inflationary pressure arising out of large investment would again have its severe impact on the poorer and weaker sections of the society.'

The Indo-Pakistan war, as stated earlier, severely dislocated the Indian economy. Foreign aid, both financial and military, was suspended by the Western countries. Trade between India and Pakistan came to a standstill. The foreign exchange situation, already acute, became worse and industries were greatly handicapped owing to the scarcity of imported raw materials, machinery and components. In the circumstances, the Fourth Five-Year Plan, as originally formulated, had to be drastically revised. The Government's economic policy was modified in certain directions to give a vigorous fillip to export promotion and import substitution, and an attempt was made to relax or remove such controls as did not serve a social purpose.

While the Shastri Cabinet provided some evidence of realism in tackling the economic problems, it did not do anything to reorganize the Planning Commission so as to make it more useful and effective. All that was done was to set up an advisory committee to the Planning Commission, known as the National Planning Council. Its formation was proposed sometime in August 1964 but it was only in March 1965 that it was actually constituted. The delay was reported to be due to disagreement among the members of the Commission about the scope and personnel of the new body. Justifying its need, the Planning Commission, in a resolution issued in March 1965, said:

'With the growth of India's economy, problems of development have become increasingly complex and it is felt that, in addition to the existing arrangements for advice and consultation, it would be useful to have a small body of specialists who would work in close and continuous association with the Planning Commission and its members.'

As regards the scope of the Council, the resolution said that 'it will arrange studies by its members, individually or in committees, of such problems as may be suggested by the Planning Commission or by the members of the Council.' The Council has seventeen non-official members, representing industry, agriculture, universities, trade unions and other interests. The Deputy Chairman of the Planning Commission is the Chairman and all members of the Commission are also members of the Council. It is doubtful, however, if the Council will be helpful to remove the deficiencies of the Commission described in chapter VIII.

REVOLT FROM THE SOUTH

Two other major events during the premiership of Shastri, which affected the prestige of the Cabinet to some extent, were the language issue and the Orissa affair.

The Constitution had laid down that from 1965 Hindi in Devanagari script would be the official language of the Government of India. It is necessary to recall that the Constituent Assembly was able to incorporate this provision in the

Constitution only by a narrow majority after a fierce controversy. There was strong opposition to it particularly from the southern States and West Bengal. The opponents of Hindi argued that it had no intrinsic merit. They were also afraid that the people of non-Hindi States would be subjected to serious disabilities and, in fact, would reduce them to the status of second class citizens, if Hindi, a mere regional language, was enthroned as the official language. There were fourteen principal languages in India and several of them, it was pointed out, were much more advanced than Hindi.

However, most people in the non-Hindi States were prepared to accept Hindi as the official language provided sufficient time was allowed for them to master it and, till then, English was permitted to be used for official purposes in addition to Hindi. In 1963 Nehru, realizing the depth of anti-Hindi feeling in the South, got the Official Language Act enacted. It provided that English would continue to be an associate official language even after Hindi was introduced from 1965. He also gave a categorical assurance, which he repeated on many occasions, that English would continue to have this status as long as the people in the non-Hindi areas desired and that no changes would be effected without their consent. This assurance from the late Prime Minister served to satisfy public opinion in the South although some, particularly the Dravida Munnerat Kazhagam—a political party that once stood for the formation of an independent Dravida State—continued to entertain fears about the impact of Hindi on other languages and on the employment prospects of the people in non-Hindi States.

The Government of India decided to introduce Hindi as the main official language from January 26, 1965. The D.M.K. took strong objection to the Republic Day, held sacred by all people, being chosen for adopting such a controversial measure. The Party, therefore, resolved to observe it as a day of mourning. The Madras Government promptly arrested its leaders to prevent disturbances. The arrests were followed by agitation. At this stage certain circulars issued by the Ministries of the Government of India regarding the use of Hindi caused widespread resentment and misgivings.

The circulars, based on instruction from the Home Ministry,

gave the impression that henceforth work in the different departments would be done mainly or even exclusively in Hindi. An attempt was made by the Home Minister to allay the fears of the non-Hindi States through a broadcast to the nation. Nanda repeated Nehru's assurance regarding the continued use of English. But at the same time, he made it clear that efforts would be made to accelerate the spread of Hindi for official purposes. So, far from quelling the agitation, Nanda's appeal intensified it.

The anti-Hindi movement in the South took a very violent turn. For nearly twenty days it created a dangerous situation. During this period fifty people were killed in police firing. Two Sub-Inspectors of police were burnt to death. Two constables were lynched. Four people died of self-immolation—three by pouring petrol on their bodies and setting fire to them and the other by taking poison. Over 10,000 people, including many students, were arrested. About 100 Government buses, and railway property worth over Rs. 1 crore, were damaged and long-distance trains remained suspended during the period of agitation. Whoever actually sponsored and directed the movement, it was clear beyond doubt that public opinion in the South was deeply disturbed over the language policy of the Government of India. West Bengal also expressed its resentment. It now looked as if the country was faced with a threat to its very integrity.

There were at least four schools of thought on the language issue. These were: (a) Hindi should be the sole official language; (b) English alone should continue as the official language for all time; (c) bilingualism for a prolonged period so as to give adequate time to non-Hindi people to study the language; (d) bilingualism on a permanent basis.

The Union Cabinet was then faced with a most difficult and explosive situation. Shastri tried to pacify non-Hindi States through a broadcast on February 11, 1965. He recalled Nehru's words on this subject and declared, 'we are most anxious to safeguard to the fullest extent the interests of non-Hindi speaking people and to avoid any inconvenience to the non-Hindi speaking States'. He promised that the Government would stand by Nehru's assurance 'fully and solemnly'. It would be honoured 'both in letter and spirit without any qualification or reservation'. He reminded the people that what was involved was the very unity of the country and so he appealed to them 'to lift this issue to a higher plane and to bestow upon it the most rational consideration'.

Shastri's broadcast, however, did not have the desired effect. Public opinion in the South felt that mere verbal promises would no longer suffice. It wanted the Constitution of India to be suitably amended. If this was not possible, at least statutory recognition should be given to Nehru's assurances. The Cabinet itself was sharply divided on this issue. C. Subramaniam, Minister of Food and Agriculture, submitted his resignation. He felt that the apprehensions of the non-Hindi States could be effectively dispelled only by appropriate parliamentary legislation. O. V. Alagesan, Minister of State for Petroleum and Chemicals, also resigned for the same reason.

Within a few days, however, both Subramaniam and Alagesan withdrew their resignation after Shastri had assured them that steps would be taken to safeguard fully the interests of the non-Hindi States.[1] The agitation was suspended. But it revealed some glaring weaknesses in the working of the Cabinet. It demonstrated to the world that the Cabinet had not carefully worked out the implications of the language policy. No attempt had been made to educate and enlighten public opinion on such a vital matter. Cabinet Ministers like Asok Sen and S. K. Patil publicly put forward certain solutions to the problem in their individual capacity, forgetting that in a parliamentary democracy the Cabinet should speak with one voice at least on major questions. Shastri did not assert himself promptly and decisively during the crisis. His action in calling a conference of Chief Ministers to consider the language question was resented by some members of his own Party. They felt that decisions should be taken by the Cabinet and not by the Chief Ministers. At a meeting of the Congress Parliamentary Party held in New Delhi on February 20, 1965, a senior Member of Bihar D. N. Tiwari,

---

[1] On March 2, 1965, a member of the Lok Sabha demanded a statement from the Food Minister on his resignation. But the Speaker ruled that it was not obligatory. He said he had no official information that Subramaniam had submitted his resignation and later withdrew it. It was an internal matter of the Cabinet. The rules of the House only provided that if a Minister tendered his resignation and it was accepted, then he had the right to make a statement.

addressing the Prime Minister, said, 'It is strange that some of your ministers talk of rethinking on the language issue while others demand that the law be amended. If your Cabinet is divided, it must be controlled. If you need our help, it is available.'

Dr Radhakrishnan, the President of India, also did not seem happy about the manner in which the Cabinet handled the language problem. In a public speech in New Delhi in February 1965 at which Shastri and many of his colleagues were present, the President said,

'Democracy is the rule of law. It is a rule of reason. It is rule by consent. We should try to achieve for all our policies as much of consent as possible. The consensus should be with us . . . But if democracy is rule by consent, we have to ask ourselves whether we did everything in our power to avert such unhealthy developments. Political wisdom consists in anticipating events, forestalling them and averting them whenever possible.'

The Government of India announced its new language policy in the first week of June 1965. Its main features were prolonged bilingualism at the Centre, that is, the use of both English and Hindi for official purposes, introduction of all the fourteen regional languages as the media for the examinations conducted by the Union Public Service Commission, and enforcement of the three-language formula at all stages of education. Under the three-language formula students all over India will have to study compulsorily English and Hindi; besides, students in non-Hindi areas will study their mother tongue while students in Hindi States will have to learn an Indian language other than their mother tongue.

A critical analysis of the language policy is beyond the scope of this study. But it is interesting and significant that the major decisions on the language problem were taken not by the Cabinet but jointly by the Congress Working Committee and the Chief Ministers of States. Of course, the Prime Minister and some of his prominent colleagues in the Cabinet are members of the Congress Working Committee; and Chagla, the Minister for Education, was also invited to attend its meetings during the discussion on the language issue. But the point to be noted is that the vital decision to introduce all the regional languages as the media for U.P.S.C. examinations was not actually favoured either by Shastri or by the Cabinet Sub-Committee which had been specially set up under the Chairmanship of Gulzarilal Nanda to consider the language question. It is believed that Kamaraj, the Congress President, played a crucial role in arriving at this decision. He was reported to have argued that since the regional languages were rapidly becoming the media of instruction and examination in the Universities it was inevitable that they should also be used for the U.P.S.C. examinations.

The new language policy was generally welcomed in the country although C. Rajagopalachari, the veteran statesman, strongly disagreed with it. 'I completely disapprove and condemn the Congress Working Committee's decision,' he said. He described it as 'a full-fledged disintegration plan.' Rajagopalachari's fears may perhaps seem exaggerated but it is an unfortunate fact that neither the Cabinet nor the Congress Working Committee nor the Chief Ministers had made a detailed and expert study of the impact of the decision on the efficiency of all-India Services or on national integration.

TRUTH ABOUT ORISSA

Another important issue that affected the Cabinet's prestige to some extent was the Orissa affair. In October 1964, a number of Opposition members from the Orissa Legislative Assembly had presented a petition to the President of India. They alleged that Biren Mitra, the Chief Minister, and B. Patnaik, Ex-Chief Minister and Chairman of the State Planning Board, had been indulging in corrupt practices of a serious nature. It was pointed out that both of them, through companies formed in the name of their wives, had amassed vast wealth. In doing so, they had also brought down the prestige of the administration. The President referred the petition to the Prime Minister and the latter set up a Sub-Committee of senior Cabinet Ministers to consider the matter. The Sub-Committee sat for several days. It came to the conclusion that Patnaik and Mitra had not personally received any pecuniary benefit from the various transactions in which they were concerned. But it found that in several transactions, improprieties were definitely involved and that the normal standards of public conduct had not been maintained. The Sub-Committee also enquired into certain allegations of corruption against the Chief Ministers of Mysore and Bihar but found them baseless. The findings of the Sub-Committee were accepted by the Cabinet. The Prime Minister thereupon advised Mitra to resign from the Chief Ministership and Patnaik from the Chairmanship of the State Planning Board. Both of them accepted Shastri's advice and submitted their resignations.

But the matter did not end there. The Opposition parties in and outside Parliament felt that the Cabinet Sub-Committee had not thoroughly and impartially examined the charges against Mitra and Patnaik and that the Cabinet had shown an anxiety to shield the Orissa leaders in order to save the prestige of the Congress. In the meanwhile, H. V. Kamath, a member of the Lok Sabha, produced in the House what he claimed to be the report submitted by the Central Bureau of Investigation which, under orders of the Home Ministry, had investigated into the Orissa affair. This lengthy document received wide publicity in the Press. Its data seemed to show that the charges against the Orissa leaders were more serious than had been admitted by the Cabinet Sub-Committee. The Opposition therefore demanded that the matter be investigated by a Judge of the Supreme Court or High Court. But the Government did not agree. It was not even prepared to admit whether the document produced by Kamath was genuine or not.

A member of the Opposition therefore tabled a no-confidence motion against Shastri's Cabinet. The resolution expressed

'want of confidence in the Council of Ministers for failing to uphold the highest standards of public conduct by a deliberate suppression of truth and by abuse of power by persons in authority in Orissa and other States and having brought into contempt the concept of constitutional government by putting party interest over national interest and attempting to shield and exonerate those who were guilty of such abuse of power and corruption.'

The resolution, of course, was defeated. Only forty-four members voted for it and 315 against it. Shastri, Chagla, the Education Minister, and Sen, the Law Minister, stoutly denied the Opposition's charges and defended the action of the Government. Shastri declared, 'I have done my duty well and honestly. I have taken every step after great care and caution and without any pressure from any quarter.' He added that there was no need for a judicial enquiry because its object—the resignation of Mitra and Patnaik —had already been achieved in far less time and with less trouble. The Central Government could do nothing more in the matter. It was for the State Government to take further action if it could be proved that there had been cases of misappropriation.

CONFIDENCE MUST COME FROM WITHIN

There was only one remarkable resignation from Shastri's Cabinet and that was by the Finance Minister T. T. Krishnamachari. He submitted his resignation on December 31, 1965 because he felt he did not enjoy the full confidence of the Prime Minister. In November 1965 about ten Members of Parliament presented a joint petition to the President of India, in the course of which they alleged that Krishnamachari had misused his ministerial position to help his sons who were engaged in business. Similar charges had been made against him by some M.P.s even during the premiership of Nehru. But Nehru thought there was no substance in these complaints. In February 1965 allegations against Krishnamachari were again made in Parliament but he emphatically denied them. Shastri also did not take notice of them. But when the M.P.s presented a petition to the President, demanding the appointment of a Commission of Enquiry, Shastri felt that he should take action since the signatories had agreed to substantiate their charges before the Commission. He, therefore, proposed to refer the matter to the Chief Justice of India to ascertain whether there was a *prima facie* case for enquiry. But Krishnamachari objected to this procedure. His stand was that the allegations were not new and that he had already refuted them categorically in Parliament. However, if necessary, Shastri himself could go through the relevant papers to ascertain if the matter called for a detailed investigation. Krishnamachari thought that by referring the petition to a third person, however eminent, the Prime Minister was indirectly indicating his lack of confidence in the Finance Minister. As he explained in his resignation letter to Shastri,

'In the ultimate analysis the question is one of confidence between the Finance Minister and his Prime Minister. As a matter of public policy, therefore, whatever the ultimate decision the Prime Minister may take, it has to be taken entirely in his individual judgment and responsibility and not arrived at as something which is based on the advice of someone else, however eminent, independent or impartial.'

Krishnamachari added: 'The relationship of the Prime Minister with the Finance Minister is of a special character and must be based on complete mutual confidence. This confidence must spring from within and should not be dependent on any sort of endorsement by any outside authority.'

Shastri's view seemed to be that if he did not ask the Chief Justice or some other impartial authority, he would not be able to convince Parliament or the country about the bonafides of the Finance Minister. He did not want to create an impression that the Prime Minister was anxious to shield his colleague for political reasons. He told Krishnamachari in his letter of December 29, 1965:

'The conclusion that there is no case for enquiry must be reached in such a manner as will carry conviction with the people and the Parliament. This could be done by taking the preliminary opinion of a person who could be relied upon to be independent and objective. Such an opinion would help me in reaching a final decision as to the need for an enquiry.'

But Krishnamachari would not agree with this procedure. He said,

'If on a matter like this, the Prime Minister says he finds himself unable to take sole responsibility for deciding whether there is a *prima facie* case for instituting an enquiry, in other words, to judge whether I have acted in any way improperly as a Minister, and if the position is that in order to carry conviction with the

F   161

people and the Parliament a preliminary opinion which could be accepted as independent and objective is essential, I am afraid it would render any working of the Cabinet system extremely difficult.'

Although Krishnamachari resigned chiefly over the procedure for enquiry proposed by the Prime Minister, it appeared from the correspondence between them, released to the Press, that the Finance Minister was unable to function effectively. In the first place, his Cabinet colleagues did not co-operate with him particularly in enforcing economy in expenditure. As he observed, 'every Minister seems to think of any proposed cut in respect of his Ministry as personal reflection on him, and thinks the only method by which this can be remedied is to eliminate completely the Finance Ministry's control.' He complained that his colleagues not only failed to co-operate with him but even tried to undermine his position. 'Some of my colleagues,' he said, 'are carrying on a daily propaganda against me and the policies of the Government for which they think I alone am responsible.' Secondly, the attitude of the State Governments was also unhelpful. Few of them made serious efforts to balance their budgets and practise fiscal discipline. This made the task of the Union Minister very difficult because the States were increasingly looking to the Centre and to the Reserve Bank for financial assistance. The States in the aggregate had a covered overdraft of Rs. 50 crores as on December 10, 1965. Their unauthorized overdraft was Rs. 117 crores on that date, the exceptions to this being West Bengal, Bihar, the U.P. and the Punjab.

Krishnamachari's resignation brought out two important aspects relating to the working of the Cabinet system: first, the Cabinet had not yet evolved a satisfactory procedure to enquire into allegations against Ministers—a procedure which was fair to the Minister concerned and which at the same time, would inspire confidence in the country about the Government's determination to root out corruption from ministerial ranks; secondly, the Prime Minister had not been able to ensure effective co-ordination among the various ministries specially those that dealt with economic subjects, and between the Centre and the State Governments.

CHAPTER XII

INDIRA AT THE HELM

Lal Bahadur Shastri died at about 1.30 a.m. on January 11, 1966 at Tashkent where he had gone to discuss Indo-Pakistan problems with President Ayub Khan. The two leaders had been brought together by the Russian Prime Minister Kosygin who urged on them to settle their differences by mutual discussions and negotiations. The talks continued for about a week and finally the historic agreement was signed by the Indian Prime Minister and Pakistan's President. Under the agreement, India and Pakistan undertook to settle their differences by peaceful means, to abide by the Charter of the United Nations, to withdraw their troops to the position they had occupied prior to August 5, 1965, to refrain from interference in each other's territory, and to resume commercial and cultural contacts which had been suspended since September 1965. The agreement was welcomed by the world's leading statesmen. They felt that a peaceful solution to Indo-Pakistan differences was essential for the economic development of both the countries and for the political stability in Asia. In India the agreement was considered as a great personal triumph for Shastri; and his sudden death by heart failure caused deep sorrow throughout the country. Even his political opponents readily conceded that Shastri had shown remarkable courage, patience and statesmanship during his premiership of about eighteen months and raised his own stature and that of India in the comity of nations.

The news of Shastri's death reached Delhi in the early hours of January 11th and immediately the President of India appointed Gulzarilal Nanda, the seniormost minister, to act as the Prime Minister until the election of the new leader. Meanwhile, the Congress President and other leaders of the party started discussions among themselves regarding the choice of Shastri's successor. It was hoped to find a leader acceptable to all sections of the party but the task proved extremely difficult.

When Nehru died, the choice of the new Prime Minister fell

on Shastri because he had the fewest opponents and therefore it was possible to elect him unanimously to the high office. But the situation on the death of Shastri was different. None of the leaders who aspired to succeed him was able to inspire confidence among all sections of Congressmen. Gulzarilal Nanda claimed that because of his seniority in the Cabinet and in view of the fact that he had twice acted as 'care-taker' Prime Minister, he should be chosen to succeed Shastri, at least until the general elections of 1967. But powerful leaders like Atulya Ghosh strongly opposed him. It appeared that Nanda had incurred the displeasure of some of his party men because of the manner in which he, as Home Minister, had conducted the campaign against corruption. Chavan, the Defence Minister, was considered as a candidate but he did not find sufficient support particularly among southern States. A suggestion was made that Kamaraj, the Congress President, should be elected Prime Minister but he did not agree. The other candidate in the field was Morarji Desai but Kamaraj and many other leaders did not like him. They were afraid that Morarji, rather strong-willed and obstinate, might not get on smoothly with the party and might not be able to mobilize popular support in the next general elections. The Congress Working Committee and most of the Chief Ministers, therefore, favoured the election of Mrs Indira Gandhi as Prime Minister. Attempts by the Congress President and other leaders to persuade Desai to withdraw and to ensure the unanimous election of Mrs Gandhi did not succeed. Desai was determined to contest. He thought that by virtue of his seniority in the Congress organization and his long ministerial and parliamentary experience, he had a stronger claim than any of his colleagues to be elected as Prime Minister. So a contest became inevitable and the Congress Party decided to conduct the election by secret ballot. A vigorous campaign was carried on by the supporters of Mrs Gandhi and Desai. Mrs Gandhi's candidature was backed up by the influential leaders of the 'syndicate', including the Congress President, as well as by most Chief Ministers. The Governor of Kerala also actively and openly campaigned for Mrs Gandhi. But she did not canvass support for herself. On the other hand, Desai strenuously conducted his own campaign. He contacted the Congress members of the Parliament by phone or in person and also issued a long statement, soliciting their votes.

In the course of his statement, Desai referred to the grim problems facing the country in respect of defence and development. The situation called for a leader who could enjoy the full support and co-operation from the members of the Congress Party. But he said that no effort was made to find such a leader. 'On the contrary,' he complained,

'those who by virtue of their positions had a special responsibility to be above personal prejudices and animus, seem to have decided that the search for unanimity should mean the elimination of all those whom they do not like. I have been greatly distressed to see how all kinds of unhealthy precedents are being set up in the effort to claim unanimous support for the choice of a few people who are in positions of authority.'

Desai said that many members of Parliament had told him of the pressures being put on them to prove their loyalty to Chief Ministers or other dignitaries in the Congress. He said,

'While it is true that every member of Parliament has to give due weight and respect to the opinions of other important people, the responsibility and the right to choose a leader rest squarely on the members of Parliament. I feel that if we surrender this right or allow it to be eroded by the use of extraneous pressures, we shall be bringing into disrespect the sacred institution of Parliament which we have accepted as the expression of the National Will as well as the great heritage of the love of freedom and liberty which has always inspired the Congress. Many members of Parliament and other public men including Ministers at the Centre and in the States have told me that this is a tendency which bodes ill for the future of democracy, in the organization and in the country and this has to be resisted.'

Desai denied he had personal fads or obsessions as alleged by his critics. All he had done was to stand firmly for whatever the organization had accepted as its goal and policy. 'I know,' he said, 'how difficult the task of the Prime Minister is. I have, therefore, agreed to offer myself as a candidate only in a spirit of humility.' At his last Press Conference prior to the poll, Desai explained that he did not favour unanimity at any cost. If it came naturally, it was good. Otherwise, unanimity brought about artificially was harmful to democracy. 'Why am I not acceptable,' asked Desai at the Press Conference. 'If artificially someone is made acceptable, he is not so. I think I am more acceptable. What have I done to justify this kind of argument? Let Kamaraj say that the organization has no trust in me. If he says so, I will give my reasons.' Desai, however, made it clear that he had no differences with Mrs Gandhi on policy. He said, 'As members of the Congress we adhere to the same programme and policy. There is no question of a difference. But there may be differences on the manner of implementation.'

The contest for the leadership was thus keen and vigorous. As the polling day came nearer, it was evident that Mrs Gandhi would win by a comfortable majority. But Desai continued to express optimism in his victory.

The Congress Parliamentary Party met at 11 a.m. on January 19 to elect its leader. Kamaraj presided over the meeting held in the Central Hall of Parliament. The Hall has acquired historic significance. It was here that the British transferred power to India and it was in the same Hall that India's Constitution was made and adopted. The total number of Congress members present at the meeting was 526—363 out of 375 from the Lok Sabha and 163 out of 176 from the Rajya Sabha.[1] Mrs Gandhi[2] and Desai were present at the meeting but both of them refrained

---

[1] The Congress Party in Parliament has a strength of 549-373 in the Lok Sabha and 176 in the Rajya Sabha. The following is the breakdown of Congress members from various States: Andhra Pradesh 31+14=45; Assam 10+7=17; Bihar 44+16=60; Gujarat 16+10=26; Kerala 6+4=10; Madhya Pradesh 26+11=37; Madras 31+13=44; Maharashtra 42+15=57; Mysore 24+10=34; Orissa 13+7=20; Punjab 13+8=21; Rajasthan 14+8=22; U.P. 60+24=84; West Bengal 22+12=34; Jammu and Kashmir 6+4=10; Delhi 5+3=8; Himachal Pradesh 4+2=6; Manipur 2+1=3; Andamans 1; Tripura 1; Nagaland 1+1=2; NEFA 1; Pondicherry 1+1=2; Laccadive Islands 1; Goa 1 and nominated members in the Rajya Sabha 4.

[2] On the morning of the polling day, Mrs Gandhi visited Raj Ghat and Shanti Vana, where Mahatma Gandhi and Jawaharlal Nehru had been cremated, and offered prayers. She then went to the former residence of Nehru, which is now a national museum, stood in silence before her father's portrait and burst into tears.

from voting. Mrs Gandhi's name was proposed by Nanda and seconded by N. Sanjiva Reddy, and K. Hanumanthaiyya of Mysore proposed the name of Morarji Desai and it was seconded by Tikaram Paliwal of Rajasthan. Mrs Gandhi secured 355 votes and Desai 169. Mrs Gandhi thus became India's third Prime Minister and also the country's first woman Prime Minister.[1]

The election went off smoothly. As Dr Radhakrishnan said in his Republic Day broadcast to the nation on January 26, 1966,

'The election was a contested one and its conduct proved a victory for sheer decency in public life. The two candidates were free from traces of bitterness or rancour. They both love the country and the ideals we cherish and our people will stand together as one in facing the tremendous tasks that await us.'

However, it is necessary to draw attention to certain aspects of the election which, from the constitutional point of view, are likely to create some unhealthy precedents. For instance, the new Prime Minister is not a member of the Lok Sabha or the Lower House of Parliament but of the Rajya Sabha or the Upper House. Although there is no provision in the Constitution debarring a member of the Rajya Sabha from being elected as Prime Minister, it would have been better if a convention had been established for choosing the Prime Minister only from the Lok Sabha. After all, it is the Lok Sabha that is the more popular and powerful of the two Houses of Parliament. Members of the Lok Sabha are chosen by direct election under adult suffrage while members of the Rajya Sabha are elected indirectly. In the circumstances, it will surely be in conformity with the spirit of democracy if the person chosen as the Prime Minister belongs to the Lok Sabha.

The role of the Chief Ministers of States in the election of Mrs Gandhi calls for some critical comments. The Chief Ministers had also a hand in the selection of Shastri as Prime Minister but at that time their participation was not conspicuous. They made their influence felt from behind the scenes. But in the election of Mrs Gandhi, the Chief Ministers played an aggressive role. Most

[1] Under the Indian Constitution, the leader of the majority party in the Lower House of Parliament is called upon by the President of the Republic to form the Cabinet.

of them not only supported the candidature of Mrs Gandhi openly but actively campaigned for her by persuading the M.P.s from their respective states to vote for her.[1] The action of the Chief Ministers was sought to be justified mainly on two grounds: first, as senior Congressmen the Chief Ministers also had a right to take part in the elections of the Prime Minister; secondly, as Chief Ministers, they had a responsibility to ensure that the person chosen as the Prime Minister was acceptable to the States. The role of the Chief Ministers was strongly defended by the Congress President. He said, in an interview to a foreign correspondent, 'Everyone has a free expression of views. Without all the States, where is the Centre? The Chief Ministers certainly represent the States. Without the States how do you have India and Parliament?'

But the Congress President was not creating a sound convention because the same political party will not always be in power at the Centre and in all the States. It is likely that in due course at least in some States, a party other than the Congress may come into power; and in such a situation, will the Chief Ministers of those States have a voice in the election of the Prime Minister? Moreover, if Chief Ministers are allowed to influence the Prime Minister's election, it may be difficult for the Central Government to exercise its authority over the States. The economic and educational development of India will depend largely on the extent to which the Centre is able to enforce a uniform policy on major issues in the national interest; and this task may become nearly impossible if the Prime Minister has to depend on the goodwill of the Chief Ministers for his or her election.

Another undesirable trend noticed in the election of Mrs Gandhi was the part played by A. P. Jain, the Governor of Kerala. Being under President's rule, Kerala had no Chief Minister and the Governor therefore was carrying on the administration. But Jain rushed to New Delhi immediately after the death of Shastri and, according to his own admission, personally campaigned for the election of Mrs Gandhi; and after the result was known, he

[1] But the Chief Ministers were not allowed to be present in the Central Hall of Parliament at the time of polling. Originally, seats had been arranged in the Hall to enable the Chief Ministers to watch the polling. But Morarji Desai objected to this procedure.

announced his resignation from the Governorship. Jain's conduct was severely censured by the Indian Press because, apart from the constitutional impropriety, he had stayed away from his State when it was passing through a serious food crisis.

The part played by Kamaraj in the election has been praised by many in India and abroad. It is true he managed the election successfully. But is it desirable for the Congress President to dominate the election in the manner he did? It is all right so long as the candidate chosen by the Congress President is accepted by the Congress Parliamentary Party. But if, as is not unlikely in future, the nominee of the Congress President is rejected by the Congress M.P.s, then, there may be an open rift between him and the Prime Minister.

The election of Mrs Gandhi as Prime Minister was widely welcomed in India and in other countries. There were however critics who strongly disapproved of the manner in which the Congress Parliamentary Party elected its leader. C. Rajagopala-chari, for instance, said that Morarji Desai had done a definite service to democracy 'by halting the downward slide of the Congress Party towards monolithic totalitarian organizational procedures.' M. R. Masani, a prominent member of the Opposition in the Lok Sabha, said, 'The action of the Congress President and the Chief Ministers in calling M.P.s from different states in small meetings and trying to commit them in advance showed a cynical contempt for the sanctity of the ballot, which is frightening.' Acharya Kripalani said that it would have added to the dignity of the Congress if it had observed in the election the democratic form of free vote. Doubts were also expressed by some Opposition leaders whether Mrs Gandhi would be able to tackle successfully the stupendous problems confronting the country.

It was, of course, true that the powerful provincial chiefs of the Congress backed up Mrs Gandhi because she was the only leader who could decisively defeat the redoubtable Morarji Desai. But that surely was not the only reason why she received the overwhelming support of the Congress Parliamentary Party. There were other factors that favoured her election. Mrs Gandhi's youth and personal charm, her long and distinguished political career, her personal contacts with the great statesmen of the world and the fact that she had closely watched India's first

Prime Minister at work for nearly eighteen years—all these also influenced her election.

Mrs Gandhi was educated at Allahabad, Viswa-Bharati, Oxford and Switzerland. In 1942, in her twenty-fifth year, she married Feroze Gandhi who later became a prominent member of the Lok Sabha. But the marriage, which was against the wishes of her father, did not prove happy and Feroze died in 1960. Despite her rather frail health, Mrs Gandhi took an active part in politics and suffered imprisonment for about a year. After the attainment of independence she held responsible posts in the Congress as a member of the Congress Working Committee as well as of several other Committees which dealt with the choice of candidates for election, disciplinary action, and so on. In 1959 she was elected the Congress President in which role she showed considerable organizing ability. It was during her tenure as the Congress President that the Communist Ministry in Kerala was overthrown. Mrs Gandhi has also taken a lively interest in cultural affairs. During Nehru's premiership her name was sometimes mentioned as a possible successor to her father. But few took the suggestion seriously because Nehru himself never favoured it and many thought that Mrs Gandhi, in view of her delicate health and lack of adequate political and parliamentary experience, would hardly make a successful Prime Minister. However, on the death of Shastri, Mrs Gandhi emerged as the only leader acceptable to the large majority of Congress M.P.s and Chief Ministers.

Mrs Gandhi submitted her list of Ministers to the President of India at 2.30 a.m. on January 24. The fact that the Prime Minister-designate was able to complete her list of ministers only in the small hours of the morning indicated, incidentally, that her task was by no means easy. (Shastri presented his Cabinet list to the President at 1.30 a.m.) Mrs Gandhi's colleagues could not readily agree among themselves either about the distribution of portfolios or the ranking of ministers. The swearing-in ceremony took place at 2.30 p.m. on January 24 at Rastrapathi Bhawan.[1]

[1] An unusual practice followed at the swearing-in ceremony was the invitation extended to the Congress President to attend it. According to C. Rajagopalachari, the swearing-in of ministers should not be a public ceremony. The ex-Governor-General observed that the oath of secrecy taken by the

The list of the Council of Ministers is given at the appendix. Mrs Gandhi's Council of Ministers consists of sixteen Cabinet Ministers, eighteen Ministers of State and seventeen Deputy Ministers. (At the time of Shastri's death, the Council was composed of fifteen Cabinet Ministers, sixteen Ministers of State and twenty-one Deputy Ministers.) The average age of Mrs Gandhi's Cabinet is 58·25. The Prime Minister is forty-eight. Sanjivayya, the Minister for Industry, is the youngest at forty-four while G. S. Pathak, the Law Minister, is the oldest at seventy.

Mrs Gandhi did not make drastic changes in the composition of her Cabinet mainly because of the general elections to be held early in 1967. Two Cabinet Ministers, Asok Sen and Humayun Kabir were dropped.[1] Three new persons were included, namely Asoka Mehta and G. S. Pathak and Fakhruddin Ahmed. Manubhai Shah, Minister of State for Commerce, was promoted to Cabinet status with the same portfolio. The senior ministers were practically left undisturbed except in the case of Sanjivayya and Sanjiva Reddy who were given Industry and Transport respectively. The Minister of Food was given additional charge of Community Development and Co-operation. Under Shastri, Iron and Steel was looked after by a Cabinet Minister but Mrs Gandhi gave this portfolio to a Minister of State. Similarly, Petroleum and Chemicals as well as Information and Broadcasting, which had been given Cabinet status under Shastri, were downgraded and given to Ministers of State.

The other important changes were the following: The Department of Company Affairs and Insurance was abolished. Company Affairs were transferred to the Law Ministry and Insurance to the Department of Revenue. The Bureau of Public Enterprises

---

Prime Minister and other Ministers would cover even communicating things to the Congress President, although the Prime Minister occupies his or her position by reason of the strength of the Congress Party. He added, 'This incident of the Congress President's presence at the swearing-in ceremony is a very disturbing symptom of the growing approximation of the Indian Government towards the Communist system, wherein the party hierarchy is above the government hierarchy and so recognized officially.'

---

[1] Mahavir Tyagi, a Cabinet Minister under Shastri, had resigned a few days earlier as a protest against the 'caretaker' Cabinet endorsing the Tashkent Agreement.

was taken out from the Department of Co-ordination in the Finance Ministry and given to the Cabinet Secretariat. The Ministry of Industry was bifurcated into the Ministry of Industry and the Ministry of Supply and Technical Development. Similarly, the Ministry of Steel and Mines was split into the Ministry of Iron and Steel, and the Ministry of Mines and Metals. The Ministries of Civil Aviation and Transport were merged to form the new Ministry of Transport, Aviation, Shipping and Tourism. The Department of Rehabilitation ceased to constitute a separate ministry. It was transferred to the Ministry of Labour, Employment and Rehabilitation.

The Union Health Ministry was re-designated as Ministry of Health and Family Planning; and its responsibility for certain town planning and development activities was transferred to the Works and Housing Ministry which was re-named as the Ministry of Works, Housing and Urban Development.

The Department of Social Security was re-named as Department of Social Welfare. Subjects relating to village industries including Khadi, handicrafts and Amber Charka, which were under the Department of Social Welfare, were transferred to the Ministry of Commerce. Similarly, subjects relating to 'Bal Bhavan' and children's museums were transferred in the Ministry of Education from the previous Department of Social Security.

Some of the changes introduced by Mrs Gandhi were well conceived. The elevation of Commerce to the Cabinet status is an indication of the great importance attached by the Government of India to export promotion. The extension of the responsibility of the Food Minister to include Co-operation and Community Development is likely to contribute to better development of agriculture. The re-designation of the Health Ministry as Ministry of Health and Family Planning is symbolic of the Government's earnestness in checking the population growth.

But certain other changes seem hard to justify. For example, the transfer of Company Affairs to the Law Ministry has been criticized because the Finance Ministry is considered to be the more appropriate agency for administering the corporate sector. The transfer of the control over the Bureau of Public Enterprises is likely to weaken the authority of the Finance Ministry over

the public sector enterprises which account for huge investments. The downgrading of Iron and Steel, Mines and Metals as
well as Petroleum and Chemicals to the Minister of State level
does not appear sound since these departments deal with subjects
of great importance to the country's economic development. It
is obvious that the re-organization of the departments has been
done more with a view to accommodating the aspirations of the
Ministers concerned rather than from the point of view of
ensuring maximum efficiency.

In her first broadcast as Prime Minister, on January 26, Mrs
Gandhi assured the people that her approach to the country's
problems was 'one of humility'. She emphasized on the urgent
need to increase production in agriculture and industry, to
achieve a greater self-reliance in many fields, to strengthen the
country's defence, to improve administrative efficiency and to
maintain peace and friendship with other nations. She said,

'We have promises to keep to our people— of work, food, clothing and shelter, health and education. The weaker and under-
privileged section of our people—all those who require special
measures of social security—have always been and will remain
uppermost in my mind.'

The world will watch with interest how India's first woman
Prime Minister tackles the many difficult problems confronting
this great country of nearly 500 million people.

CHAPTER XIII

WHAT PROSPECTS FOR INDIAN DEMOCRACY?

From the preceding chapters, it is clear that the record of the Indian Cabinet, both during and after Nehru's time, has been on the whole creditable. No one, of course, claims that the Cabinet has always done the right thing at the right time and in the right manner. But when we consider the vast size of the country and the nature of its diverse and difficult problems, the achievements of the Indian Cabinet should be regarded as praiseworthy. It has preserved the unity of the country, built up traditions of parliamentary democracy, maintained the rule of law, and tried to develop the economy through peaceful means. India's record is particularly commendable when compared with that of other Asian countries. In many of them democracy has disappeared and given way to dictatorship. Indeed, in the post-war world, few countries can boast of such a long and continuous period of political stability and democratic rule as India.

The question now arises how rapidly India will be able to progress in the coming years without impairing her democratic set-up. The great problems confronting the country at present relate to national integration, development of the economy, and improvement of administration. These issues are, of course, rela-set-up. The great problems confronting the country at present not only on the efficient working of the Cabinet but on the extent to which it is able to enlist the support and co-operation of the Opposition.

HOW STRONG IS THE UNION?

There is, of course, no immediate danger to Indian unity. But this feeling of oneness seems largely artificial, created by the Chinese aggression and the danger from Pakistan. The Constitution of India, moreover, has been amended with a view to making the demand for secession illegal. But one has only to recall the conditions prior to the Chinese invasion in October 1962 to realize the dangerous extent to which fissiparous forces had strongly entrenched themselves in strategic parts of the Indian Union. The reorganization of States on a linguistic basis had created fierce rivalries and jealousies, and in the South, the movement for secession was gathering rapid momentum.

'It has been most distressing to us,' said the States' Reorganization Commission in its report in 1956,
'to witness a kind of border warfare in certain areas in which old comrades-in-arms in the battle for freedom have been pitted against one another in acrimonious controversy, showing little appreciation of the fact that the States are but the limbs of the same body politic and that territorial readjustments between them should not assume the form of disputes between alien powers.'

The States even defied the Centre, and some Chief Ministers negotiated directly with foreign countries for getting financial and technical aid without reference to the Government of India or the Planning Commission. This unconstitutional practice was stopped only when Nehru issued a circular to Chief Ministers early in 1962, strongly deprecating such a procedure. Attempts to develop the economy through the Five-Year Plans failed to evoke popular enthusiasm. The situation became so serious that the Prime Minister had to call a National Integration Conference in New Delhi in June 1961 and set up a number of influential committees to suggest measures for preserving the unity and independence of the country. But these Committees suspended their work when, soon after the Chinese invasion, the nation displayed a strong sense of solidarity.

Apart from the external danger, the personality of Nehru had been the most powerful unifying factor. Even his fierce critics freely acknowledged his remarkable capacity to weld together the various parts and serve as an effective symbol of a united nation. K. M. Munshi, a former Minister in the Union Cabinet and now a leader of the Swatantra Party, hardly exaggerated when, in his speech at the National Integration Conference in New Delhi in

June 1961, he said, turning to Nehru who was in the Chair: 'This linguistic chauvinism can be crushed only in your lifetime. I say this, despite my political differences with you, and you know that I have never paid you an idle compliment.' But Nehru failed to strengthen the centripetal forces and place the country's unity beyond challenge.

The formation of linguistic States is now generally admitted to be a serious blunder, and the decision to make both Hindi and English as official languages at the Centre is likely, in the long run, to do great harm to Indian unity. Bilingualism may be all right as a temporary solution and it may perhaps work well even as a permanent arrangement. But in the present conditions this is unlikely. The reason is that both Hindi and English are not given the same status. Hindi is the principal language and English only an associate language. Moreover, an influential section of leadership is vehemently opposed, for sentimental reasons, to the continuation of English in any form. At the same time, public opinion in the South and in West Bengal is determined not to permit Hindi to be the sole official language. Meanwhile, the excessive importance attached to regional languages even in higher education will intensify provincial feelings and weaken national integration.

Communalism and casteism are two other obstacles to the development of democracy. Communalism, of course, is not as widespread and acute today as in the British period. Nevertheless it continues to exist in various degrees of strength in different parts of the country. Casteism too is a powerful factor in Indian politics. A study conducted by the Indian Institute of Public Administration in 1964 revealed that although caste stratifications had undergone subtle changes under the impact of socio-economic and political forces since independence, it was still a force to be reckoned with in Indian society and politics. The study pointed out that modern industrial forces, while helping to break down the barriers of caste in regard to eating, drinking and other forms of contact, had tended to bring members of the same caste together to capture the benefits of social and economic progress. Casteism, the study added, 'has a vested interest in backwardness', since it enables the people concerned to demand special treatment in terms of expenditure and reservations.

Thus the unity of India rests on insecure foundations and this fact may imperil the future of democracy. Indian history clearly shows that the country stood united in the past only when there was a strong king or emperor; and when he was succeeded by weak rulers, the provincial chiefs began to assert their independence; and disintegration set in, often followed by foreign invasion. This was what happened after the death of Asoka, Harsha and Akbar; and it may happen again, now that Nehru is gone, unless the unifying forces are effectively strengthened. It was but appropriate therefore that in his first broadcast to the nation as Prime Minister, Shastri made a fervent appeal to the people to stand united in all circumstances. He said: 'Let people in different parts of the country, however strong their feelings might be on particular issues, never forget that they are Indians first and that all differences must be resolved within the unalterable framework of one nation and one country. Let us make every endeavour to foster this feeling of oneness and to carry forward the work of national integration started with the National Integration Conference in 1961.'

STAGNANT ECONOMY — THREAT TO DEMOCRACY

The failure of the Indian economy to develop rapidly is another major threat to the future of democracy. We have seen in chapter VIII how the Five-Year Plans have not so far succeeded in improving the economic condition of the vast majority of the people. Consequently, the difference between the living standards of the people of India and those of other countries, great as it is already, is becoming more glaring. The *per capita* annual income in India in 1963 was only Rs. 303/- as compared to Rs. 12,128 in the USA, Rs. 6,030 in the UK, Rs. 6,025 in West Germany and Rs. 2,428 in Japan. A comparison of national income statistics of different countries has many limitations. But even so, it is obvious that the rate of our progress has been disappointingly slow. So, unless the economic policies are suitably adjusted and the scourge of poverty and unemployment is tackled boldly, the unity and freedom of India will be gravely imperilled. Shastri, therefore, gave high priority to the war against poverty. In his broadcast referred to above, he said:

'Of all the problems facing us, none is more distressing than that of the dire poverty in which millions of our countrymen continue to live. How I wish that I would be able to lighten the burden of poverty on our people. I cannot forget particularly the claims of the most backward sections like the Scheduled Castes and Scheduled Tribes, who had suffered neglect and had endured disabilities for many centuries. It would be my proud privilege to work for the establishment of a more just social order.'

But the outlook for economic development does not appear to be quite encouraging. The success of the Fourth Plan will depend largely on how efficiently and closely the public sector and the private sector work together in the interests of the country. But unfortunately the two sectors still seem to be engaged in a sort of cold war. The Government is determined to increase the sphere of the public sector steadily and even spectacularly. But the record of the public sector undertakings in terms of financial results has been disappointing. On a total investment of Rs. 1,026 crores as at the end of 1963-4 the net profit of public sector enterprises (other than departmental undertakings) was only Rs. 11·75 crores or 2·85 per cent. It is true that, individually, a few government enterprises have been able to show profit. But considering the public sector as a whole the performance has not been satisfactory. At the same time, the private sector is not being permitted, on ideological grounds, to expand vigorously. Excessive taxation, controls of prices, production and profits, and increasing regimentation of the economy are hampering the freedom, initiative and enterprise of the private sector. At the annual meeting of the Federation of Indian Chambers of Commerce and Industry held in New Delhi in March 1965, Lal Bahadur Shastri complained that the private sector had withheld its co-operation from the Government in tackling the difficult food problem. Asoka Mehta, Deputy Chairman of the Planning Commission, who addressed the meeting, expressed his surprise at the fact that India's industrial parliament (that is, the Federation) had expressed with one voice its disapproval of the size and scope of the Fourth Five-Year plan. He advised them 'to cast off their tattered garments

178

of pessimism and gloom and don the armour of optimism'. But the fact remains that on the eve of the inauguration of the Fourth Five-Year Plan the gulf between Government and industry remains as wide as ever. This is not conducive to rapid economic growth.

HOW TO MODERNIZE ADMINISTRATION

How fast the economy will grow will depend largely not only on the adoption of right policies but on the improvement of the administrative machinery. In this respect Nehru was not able to achieve much success. Although the first, second and third five-year plans laid great emphasis on the importance of administration, and a number of influential committees examined the problem from time to time, the administrative machinery, far from showing signs of improvement, is becoming less efficient. Year after year, the Federation of Indian Chambers of Commerce and Industry, at its annual meeting, draws pointed attention to the abnormal delays in carrying out schemes of industrial development because of the failure of the administration to cope with its growing responsibilities. At its annual meeting in March 1963, for instance, a resolution was adopted, deploring the fact that there was 'hardly any decision which the industry and trade can take without getting the approval of the authorities.' The resolution added:

'The administrative delays in the disposal of applications have been not a little responsible for procrastination and confusion. The Federation cannot help pointing out that Governmental policy seems to be influenced by considerations other than economic in the disposal of applications for expansion of existing units and establishment of new ones . . . The Federation also appeals for an impartial consideration of the root causes, which will reveal the connection between multiplicity of legislative measures, rules and regulations and administrative inefficiency, and unproductive time-consuming work all round, as also between indecisiveness and slackness in administrative machinery and the proliferation of Governmental agencies.'

179

India's civil service, on the whole, has adjusted itself to the changing situation, and it is surely more efficient than its counterpart in other Asian countries. But any failure to cope with its new responsibilities is due, firstly, to the complications arising from an increasingly regimented economy and, secondly, to the wrong relationship between minister and civil servant. Socialism in India is considered to be synonymous with nationalization of the means of production and distribution. But since proper attention is not given to the improvement of administration, socialism gets discredited, the economy stagnates, corruption grows and the people suffer. As the Planning Commission says:

'As large burdens are thrown on the administrative structure, it grows in size; as its size increases, it becomes slower in functioning. Delays occur and affect operations at every stage, and expected outputs are further deferred. New tasks become difficult to accomplish if the management of those in hand is open to just criticism.'

The relationship between the civil service and the ministers has not always been as perfect as it ought to be. Parliamentary democracy requires that ministers should concern themselves with policy matters, leaving their implementation to the services. Ministers, of course, should ensure that the policies laid down by the Cabinet and approved by Parliament are promptly and faithfully carried out, but there should be no political interference with the services in the discharge of their duties. 'The relations between a minister and his secretary,' said Disraeli, 'are, or at least, should be, among the finest that can subsist between two individuals. Except the married state there is none in which so great a confidence is involved and in which more forbearance ought to be exercised or more sympathy ought to exist.'

In India, ministers generally do not seem to appreciate the right role of the civil service in a democracy and, consequently, the civil service has been unable to perform its task fearlessly. On critical occasions, the services are reluctant to take decisions because they are not sure that ministers will not let them down.

Ministers also sometimes interfere too much with administrative details. This, for instance, is what Brecher said of Nehru:

'The fact of the matter is that Nehru is an inept administrator. Decisions are concentrated in his hands to an incredible degree, not only because of objective pressures but also because of his all-consuming interest in the pettiest of details. He lacks both the talent and temperament to co-ordinate the work of various ministries. More important, he has never shown a capacity or inclination to delegate authority. The result has been the administrative jungle which he bemoans.'

The comments of C. S. Venkatachar, a retired member of the Indian Civil Service, and a former Secretary to the President of India, are also worth quoting. He says:

'What has actually happened in Independent India is this: the civil servants are comparatively well paid and work in decent material conditions. At the same time, they are distrusted at higher levels. At district level, they are supervised by partymen of dubious virtue. The expanding nature of the functions of Government has made the civil servants more valuable than ever as specialists and scapegoats. Partymen prefer the civil service in the latter role but ministers at the Centre are disposed to be more tolerant and understanding. As you descend down the escalator from the higher regions of the Prime Ministerial Government and touch the ground floor of the district administration, you see glaring maladjustment between the democratic apparatus and the administrative machinery, marked warping of both, less efficiency and more confusion.'

Shastri, soon after he took over as Prime Minister, pledged himself to reform the administrative machinery. He said:

'The administrative organisation and its methods and processes must be modernized if it is to become an effective instrument of economic change. I shall do my best to have systematic attention paid to these major problems and I shall apply myself closely to the problem of administrative reforms in its various aspects.'

Mrs Gandhi also has expressed her determination to tone up administrative efficiency. In her first broadcast, she said:

'In economic development, as in other fields of national activity, there is a disconcerting gap between intention and action. To bridge the gap we should boldly adopt whatever far-reaching changes in administration may be found necessary. We must introduce new organizational patterns and modern tools and techniques of management and administration. We shall instil into Government machinery greater efficiency and sense of urgency and make it more responsive to the needs of the people.'

But administrative reform is not going to be easy, particularly in view of the introduction of bilingualism in the Central Government.

CRUSADE AGAINST CORRUPTION

Slackness in administration has been an important factor leading to widespread corruption. Its elimination from public life is one of the toughest problems confronting Indian democracy. In other countries also, corruption continues to flourish in various degrees. But the problem in India is somewhat different. In countries like the UK and the USA, the democratic tradition is strong, public opinion is alert and vigorous, the living standards are high, and the gap between the rich and the poor is comparatively small.

India, on the other hand, is a young democracy and the three Five-Year Plans have not succeeded in improving the living standards of the vast majority of the people. At the same time, the growth of the Press, a powerful organ of public opinion, is retarded by the severe shortage of newsprint. In the circumstances, corruption on a large scale is bound to demoralize the administration.

The nature of the problem is such as to defy an easy solution. Kautilya, that shrewd observer of human affairs, shows in his Arthasastra how difficult it is to catch the corrupt official. He says:

'Just as it is impossible not to taste the honey or the poison that finds itself at the tip of the tongue, so it is impossible for a

Government servant not to eat up, at least a bit, of the King's revenue. Just as with fish moving in water, it cannot possibly be discerned whether they are drinking water or not, so it is impossible to detect Government servants employed on official duties when helping themselves to money. It is possible to mark the movements of birds flying high up in the sky but it is not possible to ascertain the secret movements of Government servants.'

Kautilya refers to about forty ways of embezzlement: what is realized earlier is entered later; what is realized later is entered earlier; what ought to be realized is not realized; and so on.

Corruption was not a major problem in India until the outbreak of the second world war because the Government mainly confined itself to the maintenance of law and order. But the war radically changed the situation. In the anxiety to achieve victory at any cost, corruption was connived at. So the evil grew and became worse after the attainment of freedom.

The Government of independent India from the very beginning was keen to put down corruption. This will be clear from the adoption of such measures as the Prevention of Corruption Act in 1947, the appointment of a committee two years later to review the working of this Act, and another committee in 1953 to enquire into corruption in railway administration. The establishment of the Administrative Vigilance Division in 1955 and the appointment of the Vivian Bose Commission in 1956 to probe into the working of the Company Law were among the other important steps taken to check corruption. But the canker had entrenched itself so deeply into every level of administration that piecemeal measures could not deal with it effectively. The general feeling in the country was that action was being taken only against officials at the lower level and that the top men were allowed to go scot-free. Moreover, against ministers at the Centre and in the States suspected of corruption, the Government was unwilling to adopt a firm policy. This was mainly because Nehru was so loyal to his friends that he overlooked their faults; and even when serious charges were levelled against some of them, he was most reluctant to take swift and strong action. As Brecher says, 'He never thinks ill of an old colleague and rarely believes allegations of corruption. His normal response is to dismiss these charges as gossip or to question the accused directly and accept his denial without further investigation.' In 1956 C. D. Deshmukh, a former Finance Minister, suggested the appointment of an independent tribunal to enquire into corruption in high places. He said he had documentary evidence but he would place it only before an independent tribunal. But Nehru declined to do so. Ultimately, in June 1962, a Committee was set up with K. Santhanam, a Member of Parliament, as chairman, to enquire into all aspects of corruption.

The Committee submitted its report in March 1964. It made a number of important recommendations. But we shall confine ourselves only to those relating to ministers. The Committee observed that integrity in administration and public life could be maintained only if ministers at the Centre and the States set the correct example. 'The problem is difficult and delicate,' said the Committee, and added:

'There is a widespread impression that failure of integrity is not uncommon among ministers and that some ministers who have held office during the last sixteen years have enriched themselves illegitimately, obtained good jobs for their sons and relations through nepotism, and have reaped other advantages inconsistent with any notion of purity in public life. The general belief about failure of integrity amongst ministers is as damaging as actual failure. That these ministers have held office in the name of the Indian National Congress, which had evolved the highest notions of personal integrity and service under the inspiration of Mahatma Gandhi, has given rise to an exaggerated view of their failure to maintain high standards of integrity. It is a pity that neither the Congress authorities nor the great leaders who took over the Government of India realized the importance of evolving a suitable machinery and procedure for preventing and dealing with such corruption. We are convinced that ensuring absolute integrity on the part of ministers at the Centre and the States is an indispensable condition for the establishment of a tradition of purity in public services.'

The main recommendation of the Committee was that specific

allegations of corruption on the part of a minister at the Centre or a State should be promptly investigated by an agency whose findings would command respect. If a formal allegation was made by any ten members of Parliament or a Legislature in writing addressed to the Prime Minister or Chief Minister, through the Speaker or Chairman, the Prime Minister or Chief Minister should consider himself obliged by convention to refer the allegations for immediate investigation. For this purpose, the Committee suggested the appointment by the President of India of a National Panel from which an *ad hoc* committee might be selected to enquire into the charges.

The Government did not accept the Santhanam Committee's suggestion to constitute a National Panel. But in October 1964 the Government drew up a Code of Conduct for Central and State Ministers. The Code is an interesting document. Briefly the Code lays down that a person, before taking office as a Minister, should disclose to the Prime Minister or the Chief Minister, as the case may be, the details of his assets and liabilities and of any business interests of himself and of his family. The prospective minister should also sever his connections with the conduct and management of any business in which he has been interested. Moreover, as long as he remains in office, he should furnish annually to the Prime Minister or the Chief Minister a declaration regarding his assets and liabilities. The Code also lays down instructions regarding the sale and purchase of immovable property, collection of funds for political, charitable or other purposes, acceptance of gifts, and accommodation while on official tour.

The Code, however, is unlikely to be a very effective instrument for the prevention of corruption among ministers. The authority for enforcing the Code is the Prime Minister in the case of Central Ministers, the Prime Minister and the Union Home Minister in the case of Chief Ministers, and the Union Home Minister and the Chief Minister concerned in the case of State Ministers. But, as in the Biren Mitra and Patnaik case, described in the preceding chapter, the Prime Minister and the Home Minister may not always act with firmness and speed because of their understandable anxiety not to do anything, as far as possible, that is likely to damage the reputation of the Congress.

It is also significant that up to the end of March 1965 seven States had not accepted the Code. These were Assam, Madras, Mysore, Rajasthan, Jammu and Kashmir, Maharashtra, and Nagaland. One would have thought that on so important a matter like prevention of corruption, all States would promptly endorse the Code with a view to creating confidence among the public. Even at the Centre, no uniform procedure has been laid down for dealing with or determining any alleged breach of this Code. The procedure will depend on the facts and circumstances of each case. But whatever the procedure, it is extremely difficult in a parliamentary democracy like India's to devise a system that will help to eliminate completely corrupt practices on the part of Ministers. Jennings rightly remarks that 'the most elementary qualification demanded of a Minister is honesty and incorrupti- bility. It is, however, necessary that not only should he possess this qualification but also that he should appear to possess it.' In the final analysis, the only effective remedy lies in an en- lightened electorate, an alert Press, and a strong and responsible Opposition.

TOO MANY PARTIES

An efficient party system is the *sine qua non* of a parliamentary democracy. There should be at least two parties, both of them effectively organized and sufficiently strong so as to be able to form the Government when called upon to do so. It is also essen- tial that while the parties may differ from one another on many issues of national and international affairs, they should agree on fundamental principles, especially on the need to protect demo- cracy, to uphold the Rule of Law, to safeguard the independence of the judiciary, and to maintain the liberty of the individual.

But in India the party system has not developed on proper lines. For practical purposes, there are only two parties—the Congress and the Communists. The other parties are hardly of importance so far as the Central Government is concerned. The Congress, of course, has been continuously in office at the Centre ever since the attainment of freedom, and also in all States except

Kerala—where for a brief period of twenty-seven months the Communists held power. So long as Nehru lived, the Congress, with all its rivalry and groupism, was able to function as the largest and the most efficient party in the country. The manner in which the Congress tackled the problem of succession after the death of Nehru and Shastri has helped to enhance its reputation; and even if in the next few years its overwhelming majority in the Lok Sabha is reduced to some extent, it will continue to remain the largest political party for a long time to come.

It seems, however, odd and unfortunate indeed that the world's largest democracy has no effective Opposition. Although there are a number of political parties opposed to the Congress there is none which is sufficiently organized so as to be able to function as an alternative government. The Praja Socialist Party was wound up in June 1964 when about a thousand members, including Asoka Mehta, resigned and joined the Congress, while the rest of its members merged themselves with the Socialist Party. But the latter under Lohia's leadership has hardly any influence in all-India politics or even at the regional level. The Swatantra Party, which came into existence in 1960, seems to have created a good impression, but like the Congress, it suffers from a dearth of talent. C. Rajagopalachari, its founder, commands considerable respect throughout the country but, in view of his advancing age—he is now eighty-six—he will be unable to provide effective leadership. Other Swatantra leaders like M. R. Masani and N. G. Ranga are competent parliamentarians but they have yet to acquire all-India status. The Jan Sangh is powerful in certain areas like Rajasthan, but is most unlikely to grow as a responsible opposition because of its rather communal outlook.

The Communists perhaps could have emerged as a powerful Opposition party. But at present they are sharply split into two —the Right Wing and the Left Wing. The differences between the two arose after the Chinese aggression of India in 1962. While the Right Communists disapproved of Chinese policy towards India, the Left Communists thought that it was India that had committed agression against China! But both sections have no firm faith in parliamentary democracy. Both look upon the legislature merely as a convenient instrument with which to capture power, if possible, in course of time. Moreover, neither section fully identifies itself with the interests of India. The Right Communists look up to Moscow for inspiration and instruction and the Left Communists to Peking.

The Left Communists have been even accused of conspiring with China to overthrow the Government of India. Towards the close of 1964, several leading members of the Left Communist Party were arrested; and although some of them were elected to the Kerala Legislative Assembly in the mid-term elections in February 1965, the Government of India declined to release them. The Government's view was that these leaders were detained without trial because they constituted a grave risk to India's security. Nanda, the Union Home Minister, disclosed in the Lok Sabha on March 12, 1965 that the Left Communists had been instructed by Peking to prepare for a violent revolution in India. The methods suggested included the creation of secret cells, arms dumps and training in guerilla warfare.

The Home Minister also stated that the Left Communists had received 'considerable financial resources' from China and used them for various purposes. Nanda defended their detention without trial on the ground that the country was passing through an Emergency and therefore it was not possible to resort to the normal legal procedure to deal with the Left Communists.

It is difficult to say at this stage how long the Communist Party will continue to remain divided as at present. Some observers point out that the differences between the two groups are not really of a serious nature and that at heart they are inspired by the same ideology. It is stated that the Right Communists fully supported the Left Communists in the elections to the Kerala Assembly in February 1965.[1]

It is thus clear that there is no prospect in the near future of the emergence of a united Opposition. But then is it really necessary for the successful working of democracy? The late K. M. Panikkar said that while a powerful Opposition, capable of providing an alternative government, was undoubtedly desirable

[1] The pro-Peking Communists won forty out of the 133 seats in the Kerala Legislative Assembly.

188

in a democratic system, it was by no means essential. 'What is necessary,' he said, 'for a proper functioning of democracy is freedom of criticism, a strong and effective public opinion, a vigilant and independent Press, and a public alive to its rights.' Panikkar was right in saying so but then the Opposition parties tend to become obstructive when they know they have no chance of being entrusted with power.

How deeply the Opposition parties in the Indian Parliament are divided among themselves was illustrated clearly during the historic no-confidence resolution, the first ever brought forward against the Union Cabinet in August 1963. The motion was sponsored by seventy-two members of the Lok Sabha, but it was defeated: 346 members voting against it, sixty-four in favour and twenty-four abstaining. M. R. Masani claimed that although the Opposition did not succeed in getting the resolution passed, it did help to highlight the fact that the Congress did not enjoy as much confidence in the country as the voting seemed to indicate. He said, 'As Acharya Kripalani pointed out a year ago, only 44·72 per cent of the electorate voted for the Congress Party in the last general election. It got 361 seats. I have calculated as accurately as I could, in respect of the members who stood up in support of this motion the other day, that the parties, groups, and elements they represent polled in all forty-five million—39 per cent of the electorate in this country. If we had a system of proportional representation such as is common in many democratic countries in the world, it would be not seventy-two but 316 as opposed to your 361. Let us realize that nearly 40 per cent of the country is behind this vote of no-confidence and that the position has changed further in the last twelve months. The Chinese attack and our disastrous defeat, the gold control order, the last budget, and rising prices have further shifted public opinion as recent by-elections have shown.'

Masani's mathematics may be correct but the fact remains that the Opposition parties themselves do not have much in common. The resolution merely expressed lack of confidence but it did not specifically mention a single reason because, as a commentator observed, 'to accommodate the seventy-two sponsors, seventy-two conflicting reasons would have had to be given.'

QUORUM AND DECORUM

It is not surprising then that the Indian Parliament has not been able to conduct itself as effectively as, for example, the House of Commons. No doubt, as compared to the legislatures in other Asian countries, the record of the Indian Parliament has been commendable; and credit for enhancing its reputation should go largely to Nehru. Of Churchill it was said that 'he loved England with the passionate enthusiasm which Pericles felt for Athens and he trusted the House of Commons as no one else.' That could also be said of Nehru in relation to India and her Parliament.

Nehru was very regular in attending the sessions of Parliament, and he always treated it with great respect, and zealously tried to maintain and enhance its prestige. How Nehru conducted himself as a parliamentarian was thus described by Sardar Hukum Singh, Speaker of the Lok Sabha, in the course of his tribute to the late Prime Minister. 'Personally,' said the Speaker,

'it was a pleasure to see Nehru enter the Lok Sabha. Nehru would walk to his seat with elegance. He would give the utmost respect to the Chair. He was the first to rush to the House when the quorum or division bell was rung, provided he was in the precincts of Parliament. He used to follow the discussions carefully. His answers to questions were straight and full of information. He was always eager to give the fullest information and many a time supplemented the answers given by other ministers, if he thought the information was not adequate. He possessed detailed information about the administration and was never hesitant to share it with Parliament. Nehru kept certain standards and had left many wholesome traditions in democracy. It would be difficult to find a greater democrat than Jawaharlal. He could listen to criticism against him with patience and tolerance and could reply without rancour.'

But it is a fact that the Indian Parliament is not in a position to cope with the vast and complicated problems that confront the nation. Elections under adult suffrage have adversely affected the quality of membership.[1] In the Lok Sabha, consisting of about 500 members, there are hardly a dozen who are very well informed on economic matters, and can contribute usefully to the debates on vital issues. The quorum of the Lok Sabha is only fifty but it has always been a difficult task for the Speaker to get this minimum attendance.[2] Even when Nehru made important speeches, the attendance was not more than 200 to 300. The maintenance of discipline has been another delicate problem. Walk-outs on the slightest provocation and a tendency to defy the Chair have been too common. And the inability of a large number of members to understand either English or Hindi impedes seriously the efficient working of Parliament.

ON THE PRIME MINISTER—A HEAVY RESPONSIBILITY

Indian democracy thus has many serious shortcomings such as inefficiency in administration, glaring economic inequalities, and the absence of an effective and responsible Opposition. But there is no cause for despair about the future of democracy, provided

[1] In April 1964, H. V. Kamath moved a resolution in the Lok Sabha for prescribing a minimum qualification and an upper age limit for candidates to the Lower Houses of Parliament and State Legislatures. The resolution said that a candidate should not be above seventy-five years of age and should have in the case of the Lok Sabha passed at least a secondary education test and in the case of State Assemblies, a primary education test. The resolution, however, met with stout opposition and was rejected.

[2] The Cabinet was put to great embarrassment on April 27, 1964, when the Constitution (Seventeenth Amendment) Bill failed to secure in the Lok Sabha the requisite number of votes at the introduction stage. The Bill sought to allow State Legislatures to initiate measures of land reform where difficulty was being experienced as a result of judicial interpretation. Under the law, a constitutional amendment Bill has to be passed at all stages by a majority of the total membership of the Lok Sabha and not less than two-thirds of those present and voting. The Lok Sabha has 510 members and a minimum of 256 votes is required to pass every motion. But when the motion for consideration of the Constitutional (Seventeenth Amendment) Bill was put to the vote, there were only 206 in favour.

Also consider the following report which appeared in the *Hindu* of June 24, 1964: 'In a speech in Madras on June 23rd, Professor M. Ruthnaswami, a member of the Rajya Sabha, called for a public agitation to ensure greater attendance of Members of Parliament and Ministers in the House. Ruthnaswami said not more than ten or fifteen members of about 200 in the Rajya Sabha were present in the House at a time, while in the Lok Sabha the number averaged thirty to forty out of about 500. He said that the members' lack of interest in the proceedings of the House was depressing.'

the Congress, as the most powerful organization, sets its house in order and gives the right leadership to the country. If Congress concentrates its attention on having a clean and efficient administration and provides the people with their elementary necessities like food, clothing and shelter, it will have rendered the greatest service to democracy. The achievement of self-sufficiency in food is, after all, relatively a simple task—it is mainly a matter of effective co-ordination of the various agencies both in the Centre and in the States connected with the development of agriculture. The provision of adequate clothing should not be difficult, considering the fact that our cotton textile industry is the second largest in the world, next only to that of the United States. The problem of housing also is not hard to solve since most of the building materials are available within the country. What is required is that economic policies should be divorced from ideological bias, and they should be implemented with speed and vigour; and a sincere effort should be made to obtain the co-operation of private enterprise which hitherto has been kept at arm's length for political reasons.

The Prime Minister should ensure that the Cabinet works as a well-knit team and that ministers do not speak with different voices, particularly on major issues. The Prime Minister should also avoid the temptation to take important decisions without consulting Cabinet colleagues. Nehru sometimes did so but his position was different. As Byrum E. Carter points out, the practice of some Prime Ministers acting without Cabinet authorization is 'unusual and not without danger' because such action impairs Cabinet unity. He says, 'A Prime Minister who has such proclivities will do well to restrain them. Each incident further intensifies the strain on the thread which holds the Cabinet together, thus endangering its stability and the security of the Prime Minister in his place.' According to Attlee, a Prime Minister to be successful should function through a minister. He explained to his biographer, Francis Williams: 'A Prime Minister ought to keep his hand on the pulse and know how his ministers are doing, of course, but he must not interfere and overrule a minister.' Such a policy enabled Attlee to function effectively and at the same time enjoy much leisure. As he said, 'I read the whole of Gibbon when I was Prime Minister just at week-ends or at Chequers. I saw more of my family when I was at Number 10 than ever before or after.'[1]

There should also be closer co-operation between the Cabinet and the Congress Parliamentary Party on the one hand and between the Prime Minister and the Congress President on the other. In recent months there is an increasing tendency on the part of some senior Congress leaders to attack the Government openly either in Parliament or outside. For example, Mrs Pandit, sister of Nehru, in her maiden speech in the Lok Sabha in March 1965 strongly criticized the Government, and the Prime Minister in particular, for weakness and vacillation in dealing with domestic issues and foreign problems. She described the Prime Minister as 'a prisoner of indecision'. V. K. Krishna Menon also attacked the economic policy of the Government and described the Central budget of 1965-66 as 'a rich man's budget'. Shastri was hurt by these open attacks on his leadership. Addressing a meeting of the Congress Parliamentary Party on April 2, 1965, Shastri said, 'What is happening these days is very painful to me. If we do not realize our responsibilities, we cannot deal with the Opposition. In Parliament, in future, we should be more careful. We are passing through critical times,' Shastri added, 'What is this propaganda about indecision? It hurts me. We should not harm the party. The party has been consulted often and we meet usually once a week.' The personal relationship of Shastri and Kamaraj, the Congress President, continued to be quite cordial and the two were able to work together in close co-operation.

The Cabinet system of government under Mrs Gandhi and her successors may not work exactly as it did under Nehru and Shastri. Changes in the methods of working are bound to take place, depending largely on the personality of the Prime Minister. Even in England, the Cabinet system today works in a somewhat different manner as compared to a few years ago. On

[1] Consider, in this context, Shastri's remarks at a meeting in New Delhi on March 20, 1965. He said that he had read a large number of books on various subjects while in jail, but in recent years he had hardly any time for reading. Turning to a Member of Parliament who belonged to an Opposition party the Prime Minister said, 'perhaps I will find time for reading if his party comes into power'. The M.P. said, amidst laughter, 'I will then put you into jail.'

account of vast changes in the economic and political situation in the post-war period, power has now passed from the House of Commons into the hands of the Prime Minister and the party. The House of Commons seems to have become 'merely a forum for debate between well-disciplined political parties.' As an example of the waning power of the House of Commons, we may cite the appointment of Sir Alec Douglas-Home as Britain's Prime Minister. When in November 1963 Harold Macmillan was compelled to give up his Prime Ministership because of ill-health, he advised the Queen to send for Lord Home to form the Government. Lord Home accepted the Queen's invitation and relinquished the earldom. Thereby he ceased to be a member of the House of Lords and, at the same time, he was not a member of the House of Commons. Thus for the first time in history, Britain had for a few days a Prime Minister who was a member neither of the House of Lords nor of the House of Commons.

As R. H. S. Crossman says, in his introduction to Bagehot's *The English Constitution* :

'The post-war epoch has seen the transformation of the Cabinet government into Prime Ministerial government. Under this system, the hyphen which joins and the buckle which fastens, the legislative part to the executive part becomes one single man . . . In so far as ministers feel themselves to be agents of the Premier, the British Cabinet has now come to resemble the American Cabinet.'

Crossman, however, adds that 'the old doctrine of collective Cabinet responsibility is scrupulously maintained and enforced, even though many of the decisions for which members must assume responsibility have been taken above their heads and without their knowledge.'

In India also, whatever changes may take place in the coming years in the Cabinet personnel and procedure, it is clear that it must function strictly on the basis of joint responsibility if the nation is to make any progress. There will be no unity or discipline in the country if the Cabinet remains divided and, worse, makes its dissensions widely known. But collective responsibility is not an easy system to operate, especially in a vast country like India where parliamentary democracy has yet to take firm root. As Jennings says, 'collective responsibility assumes the team spirit of rugby football, or a well-drilled dramatic cast.' Even so, it should not be difficult to work on this principle, provided the electorate chooses leaders of ability and integrity who will always conduct themselves in the best interests of the country.

APPENDIX

MRS GANDHI'S COUNCIL OF MINISTERS AS ON JANUARY 24, 1966

CABINET MINISTERS

1.	Mrs Indira Gandhi	*Prime Minister and Minister of Atomic Energy*
2.	Gulzarilal Nanda	*Home Affairs*
3.	Jagjivan Ram	*Labour, Employment and Rehabilitation*
4.	Swaran Singh	*External Affairs*
5.	S. K. Patil	*Railways*
6.	Y. B. Chavan	*Defence*
7.	N. Sanjiva Reddy	*Transport, Aviation, Shipping and Tourism*
8.	C. Subramaniam	*Food, Agriculture, Community Development and Co-operation*
9.	Sachindra Chaudhari	*Finance*
10.	Satyanarain Sinha	*Parliamentary Affairs and Communications*
11.	M. C. Chagla	*Education*
12.	D. Sanjivayya	*Industry*
13.	Asoka Mehta	*Planning*
14.	Manubhai Shah	*Commerce*
15.	G. S. Pathak	*Law*
16.	Fakruddin Ahmed	*Irrigation and Power*

MINISTERS OF STATE

1.	J. L. Hathi	*Home Affairs*
2.	A. M. Thomas	*Defence*
3.	Dinesh Singh	*External Affairs*
4.	C. P. Poonacha	*Transport, Aviation, Shipping and Tourism*
5.	P. Govinda Menon	*Food and Agriculture, Community Development and Co-operation*

6.	Dr Ram Subhag Singh	*Railways*
7.	Bibhudendra Misra	*Industry*
8.	B. R. Bhagat	*Finance*
9.	C. R. Pattabhiraman	*Law*
10.	Mehr Chand Khanna	*Works and Housing*
11.	T. N. Singh	*Iron and Steel*
12.	O. V. Alagesan	*Petroleum and Chemicals*
13.	Raghuramiah	*Technical Development, Supply and Social Security*
14.	Dr Sushila Nayyar	*Health and Family Planning*
15.	Raj Bahadur	*Information and Broadcasting*
16.	Dr K. L. Rao	*Irrigation and Power*
17.	Jagannath Rao	*Labour, Employment and Rehabilitation*
18.	S. K. Dey	*Mines and Metals*

DEPUTY MINISTERS

1.	P. S. Naskar	*Home Affairs*
2.	Shah Nawaz Khan	*Labour, Employment and Rehabilitation*
3.	Sham Nath	*Railways*
4.	Shyam Dhar Mishra	*Defence*
5.	Anna Saheb Shinde	*Food, Agriculture, Community Development and Co-operation*
6.	L. N. Mishra	*Finance*
7.	V. C. Shukla	*Parliamentary Affairs and Communications*
8.	Bhakt Dharshan and	
9.	Dr (Mrs) Soundaram Ramachandran	*Education*
10.	D. R. Chavan	*Planning*
11.	Shafi Qureshi	*Commerce*
12.	B. C. Bhagavati	*Works and Housing*
13.	P. C. Sethi	*Iron and Steel*
14.	Sardar Iqbal Singh	*Petroleum and Chemicals*
15	Mrs Maragatham Chandresekhar	*Social Security*
16.	B. S. Murthy	*Health and Planning*
17.	Nandini Satpathy	*Information and Broadcasting*

BIBLIOGRAPHY

The British Impact on India, Percival Griffiths (Macdonald)
India Wins Her Freedom, Maulana Azad (Orient Longmans)
I Meet Rajaji, Monica Felton (Macmillan)
Transfer of Power in India, V. P. Menon (Orient Longmans)
The Viceroy and Governor-General of India, A. B. Rudra (Oxford)
President Prasad—A Biography, K. L. Punjabi (Macmillan)
The Indian Constitution in the Making, B. N. Rau (Orient Long-
mans)
Fundamentals of Planning in India, V. T. Krishnamachari (Orient
Longmans)
Nehru : A Political Biography, Michael Brecher (Oxford)
Indian Administration, Asok Chanda (Allen and Unwin)
Introduction to the Constitution of India (Third Edition), Durga Das
Basu (S. C. Sarkar & Sons)
The President under the Indian Constitution, K. M. Munshi
(Bharatiya Vidya Bhawan)
Cabinet Government, W. I. Jennings (Cambridge)
The British Cabinet System, A. B. Keith (Stevens)
The British Cabinet, John P. Mackintosh (Stevens)
The English Constitution, Walter Bagehot, Introduction by R. H. S.
Crossman (Collins)
The British Constitution, J. S. Dugdale (Brodie)
Government and Parliament, Herbert Morrison (Oxford)
A Prime Minister Remembers, Francis Williams (Heinemann)
The Office of Prime Minister, Byrum Carter (Faber)
The Decline and Fall of Lloyd George, Beaverbrook (Collins)

INDEX